AFTER THE BRIDGE

Andrew J Field

Published by Hit the North
26 Mill Wharf
Tweedmouth
Berwick upon Tweed
Northumberland
TD15 2BP

The moral right of the author has been asserted. A catalogue record for this book is available from the British Library.

ISBN: 978-1-9999826-8-3

Also
Without Rules
All Down the Line

www.afterthebridge.co.uk

Dedicated to Anthony and Janis Field...

Special thanks to
Stephanie Glencross, David Hallett, Emma Houghton, Martin Fletcher, Anne Foster, Phil MacDonnald, Sandra Mangan, Laurent Moitrot, Danuta Reah, Simon Rowberry & Katie Vandyck...and the doctors, Catherine & Anne

'Nothing is inevitable until it happens.'
A. J. P. Taylor

Slava Ukraini! Heroiam Slava!
(Glory to Ukraine, Glory to our Heroes)

www.kyivindependent.com

HIT THE NORTH

BEFORE
WEDNESDAY 4TH MAY 2022

The clock on the Audi dash said five thirty in the morning. Outside, patchy sea fret wafted across the estuary. One second foggy, the next clear. At eleven, a customer in Hull was going to be disappointed his new secondhand car never arrived.

A short walk would take him to the middle of the Humber Bridge. He had driven over many times, but never crossed on foot. This would be his first and last time, once he had completed his goodbye morning stroll.

A black leather jacket lay on the passenger seat. He would put it on when he left. Strolling around in black jeans, white tee and deck shoes before sunrise was a jumper red light. On the radio, the UK cost of living crisis, the potential Supreme Court reversal of US abortion rights and Russian war crimes in Ukraine mirrored his doom and gloom mood.

He grimaced: life had left him a dried-out shell of the man he had wanted to be. A great idea for a song, but Springsteen had already written it. The Boss knew how to spin the misery coin. Not that he identified with Bruce's liberal-bleeding-heart. His childhood hero was Robert Mitchum. Old Bob boasted he had three expressions when he acted: look left, look right and look straight ahead. Never whinged about anything. Simply carried on working, smoking and drinking, until lung cancer killed him stone dead, so the legend went. Never took himself too seriously.

He opened the glove compartment. A Marlboro Red soft-top pack contained two stale tabs. He had stopped smoking the day his wife took everything he owned, including his self-esteem. He fancied one. Except there were rules about chuffing in the motor. He tucked them into his tee sleeve, like white-middle-class people did when they played at working-class-blue-collar cool. Every macho actor had an inner Brando fighting to be released.

Yesterday, a Scottish TV and film literary agent had rejected him. Her automated email said his script didn't have a market. Maybe his work was shit, but he deserved a face-to-face. He wasn't a slush pile gimp. She knew him. They had supped wets, shared laughs and splashed juices when he was almost famous. Perhaps he was getting what he had always deserved. Tomorrow belonged to today, except when it didn't. The future was unwritten, apart from when it was. It was what it was, until it wasn't. Huh.

'Come on, don't be a wimp. What would Bob do?' He got out of the car. Forgot to put on the black leather jacket. Soon it would be immaterial what he was wearing. He strode out towards the bridge's centre, assumed it was the best place to jump. 'March on, dogs of war,' he said to himself, misquoting an ancient Alex Harvey lyric. Anyone watching would think he was the incoherent drunken barfly at chucking out time. Every pub had one. He wasn't going to waste the rest of his life waiting to be that man.

He heard footsteps and slowed. Saw a woman emerge from the mist. She was wearing a tee, and jeans tucked into knee-high black boots. Why was she out so early or up so late? Maybe she was a hooker and lifts back to her Hull Arena pitch weren't part of the sex-for-cash deal?

Who was he kidding?

Sex was the last thing on her mind. She was a jumper, surely. Like him. Interrupting his show. It was hard enough to throw himself off a bridge, without an audience scoring him for artistic interpretation.

She smiled as they passed. He walked several steps, then they both stopped and turned. She was nearly six foot tall. He was six two. She had *Ziggy Stardust* red hair. Pale skin. Wore a cotton *CUTE BUT 101% PSYCHO* tee. She resembled the words, stunning, but off her tits. Probably an addict.

'You planning the same as me?' she asked. He was too busy catching flies to respond immediately. A beat or two passed. Gulls squawked. The river

2

flowed. The rising sun warmed up the rose-pink sky.

For a moment, he pictured his ex-wife Caroline standing there, before pregnancy, motherhood and a religious cult saved her from her own tedious junkie soap opera. 'What's it to you, if I am?'

'I was here first.'

'Go on, I'll follow you in,' he said.

But she didn't go and nor did he. 'You first,' she said, and politely stepped aside.

'You'll freeze to death, save you jumping,' he said.

'You're a real comedian,' she quipped back.

'Actually, a part-time actor and sometime comic, I deliver cars to make ends meet,' he joked, and pulled the soft-top pack from his tee sleeve. Shook the pack. Tried and failed to place the accent. 'Smoke? I haven't got a lighter.'

She grabbed a tab and produced a Zippo lighter from her jeans. Flicked the gold metal top. A flame danced in front of them. They sparked up. Drew the smoke deep into their lungs. He coughed. She inhaled deeply and slowly exhaled. 'Were you famous?'

A good question. Was he ever really famous? 'In my youth, I was Vic Savage, the lead singer, lead guitarist and chief songwriter for the post-punk band Savaged by Sheep. We had two hits. Probably best known for playing tough-guy TV cop Billy Whyte in *Northern Filth*. Bloody bugger typecast me out of a serious acting career. Casting directors never saw me as a romantic or comedic lead. I grew a hipster beard. Nothing changed. You?'

'Crime fiction nobody wants to buy.'

'That's a shame,' he said.

'I'd earn more filming myself masturbating for masturbators.'

'Wanking for wankers? Why didn't I think of that indignity.' He laughed at the postmodern irony. There was always money in sex.

She was perfect honey-trapper material. 'More a humiliation, in my book. Do you have a name?'

'Owen. Owen Chard. 53. Failed husband and father. There's a long list of people I've disappointed, in the sack and everywhere else.'

'Becky. Becky Letts. 27. Recently widowed, failed crime fiction writer, porn slag.'

'Sorry about your husband,' Owen said, without asking how her significant other had died. He didn't want to discover Becky had killed hubby and was about to be arrested.

'Shit happens,' Becky said, and kicked a small stone into the dark water below. 'Here today, gone tomorrow.' She kicked another stone off the bridge. 'Happy one minute. All alone the next. Well, not alone exactly.'

'Me too,' Owen said, impressed by the way she rolled meaningless clichés off her tongue. Nobody would miss him. That boat sailed when his ex said he'd failed as a husband and a father. Several ships had passed in the night since, but none docked for more than a couple of months before heading off for more exciting adventures.

They looked at each other. Two lost souls about to top themselves.

Becky blew smoke rings and watched them expand and disperse into the fret. Her impassive face broke briefly into a smile while she toyed with them. Owen was glad she found it funny. He was thinking of ways they could commercialise sex. 'This is horny,' said Becky. 'Extreme heights excite me. Free-falling into the unknown is on my bucket list. Yours?'

Was Becky day release? Had a careless care worker left the door unlocked? She was about to kill herself and was behaving like she was descending into the Grand Canyon on an adventure holiday. Addicts were irrational once the drugs dominated their lives. He knew from personal experience. From the corner of his eye, Owen saw flashing lights on the north side. 'I'd drive an Aston Martin to Norway's Lofoten archipelago. Drink wine under the midnight sun with a beautiful woman with striking red hair and light blue-green eyes,' he said. He had a plan to delay death and exploit her physical assets.

'Enough bullshit. Empty words.'

'We don't have to jump,' said Owen, and reached for her cold hand. 'Why not make our bucket lists come true?'

'I'm skint. And you can't even afford a coat.'

'You can't afford a bra!' He half smiled and she half grinned and sucked harder on her cigarette. 'We could combine our talents and earn some easy money.'

'How?'

Owen had to make his elevator pitch fast. She was going over as soon as the fag was stubbed out. 'We honey-trap married men in hotels,' he replied. Dull PAYE men would want a girl like her. Would dream about a girl like her. Would want to fuck a girl like her. Until they puffed the dust. Consumed by guilt, they'd cough up two grand to save their marriages and keep their pensions. He squeezed Becky's hand and shuffled his body between her and the barrier. 'Split the cash fifty/fifty after expenses.'

'How's that work? I seduce, you bully?'

'We pretend we're married, and they pay for our silence.'

'After they fuck me?'

'If we get our timing right, just foreplay, a bit of touching, snogging, cock teasing.'

'Before you burst into the room and scare the shit out of them?'

'We'll make a great team,' said Owen.

'Are you that hard? That tough? That macho?'

'I am Billy Whyte. Or Billy Whyte is me. One of the two. I'm a convincing nut-job when I put my mind to it.'

'What happens when we get caught?'

'Think *Butch & Sundance. Thelma & Louise. Bonnie & Clyde.*'

'They all died,' Becky said. 'We should join them.' She took one last puff on the cigarette and flicked the butt over the rails.

'We've got company,' he said. Honey-trapping was high-risk, but it was a better than the big sleep. Owen hugged her as she lunged. Elbows dug into his ribs. Arms locked around her body.

'Let me go.'

'I can't,' Owen said, and knew he could. Pretend at the inquest she had caught him by surprise. Sob in the dock.

'My choice.'

'My conscience.' Becky bit his arm. Pain shot through his body. He retaliated by pinching her left nipple. 'They'll blame me for your death. Owen Chard will be a social outcast.'

'Nobody cares about us.' Becky bit him again and flailed her head into his face. He stayed low, hoping a lucky hit didn't damage expensive porcelain teeth he couldn't afford to repair. She grabbed his testicles. He kicked her legs, she fell to the ground and he landed on top. She lay motionless. 'Break my neck, please.'

'Stay down,' Owen hissed into her left ear, his right exposed. He waited for teeth to bite, but by some fluke, he'd knocked the fight out of her.

A bridge patrol vehicle pulled up, a middle-aged patrol officer with a comb-over wound down his window. 'What are you two doing?'

'We're celebrating,' Owen said, knowing all good lies have truthful foundations. 'We've just got engaged and heights make her horny.' Owen picked himself up. He grabbed Becky's hand and lifted her from the cold stone. The adrenaline rush was over. The fight had exhausted him. He wouldn't be able to stop her if she tried again.

'You're bleeding,' said the patrolman.

'Sorry officer,' Becky said, looked at Owen, and rubbed her left breast. 'That really hurt. My boobs are sore enough already without you tearing my bloody nipple off.'

The patrol driver stared at her with sad, lustful eyes. 'Where's your car parked? I'll give you a lift.'

'Down by the bridge car park. An Audi with dealer plates,' said Owen.

'Climb in the back,' said the patrolman.

Becky got in first. Owen followed. She whispered for his ears only. 'No stupid questions. No fuck-buddy games. No falling in love.'

'OK,' he said. 'Keep everything skin deep. Nobody gets hurt.'

Becky nodded and reached into the top of her left boot. She pulled out a flick knife and placed it between her legs. He heard a click, saw cold steel shoot upwards. 'In case you're wrong and you need to intimidate men.'

'What about you?'

'I've got my own.'

Owen took the blade and closed it, realised *CUTE BUT 101% PSYCHO* could have stabbed him anytime. He was too yellow and weak to kill himself, unlike his TV alter ego, Billy Whyte. Becky was dangerous and unpredictable, like all addicts. One minute up, one minute down. One minute your best friend and lover, the next cutting your throat. Kept you on your toes, kept you real, until fate called last orders.

Wednesday 8th June 2022
One

Ed Boucher had one eye glued on the pretty young girls walking across Manchester Piccadilly station's concourse. The other was on the Daily Telegraph cryptic crossword. In his opinion, northern women were a definite step or two down from London girls, lacked their glamorous grace, sophistication and intelligence.

Same could be said about the two cities. Despite huge digital billboards promoting Saturday's heavyweight boxing bout, million-pound skyscraper apartments knocking on heaven's door and Boohoo's super-fast online fashion, Manchester was the poor relation.

Officially, Ed was here in his capacity as a Cabinet Office nominations assessor. John Budd, a brain-damaged police hero, was in line for the Queen's highest civilian bravery medal, named after her father, King George. The off-duty Manchester detective was seriously injured a year earlier preventing the kidnapping of a rich Arab's wife. Ed's job was to confirm John Budd satisfied the George Cross's strict criteria. He would speak with Greater Manchester's chief constable, Sir Richard Hurst, who had recommended Budd for the gong. He would discuss the chief's personal statement and carry out informal financial and criminal background checks to make sure neither the Royal family nor the government were embarrassed.

Unofficially, Ed was supplementing his civil service pay and army pension with crisis management PR. In his spare time, Ed disappeared sex abuse allegations. Ed's granddaughter and co-conspirator, Alice Lamb-Percy, was active in the online abuse community and regularly befriended victims. Once she gained their trust, she would pass on their gruesome stories to Ed. He would contact the perpetrators and tell them financial compensation for the abused would protect their reputations. This gig was different. Ed and Alice were operating a couple of hundred miles from their Home Counties comfort zone. Ed had a letter saying John Budd was a rapist. If it went public, Budd could kiss his George Cross goodbye. The chief constable had the clout to make the sex claims vanish.

Ed checked his watch; Alice was an hour overdue. Being late was not unusual, she was tardy. If she'd stayed in the Marines, like Ed had advised, that would have resolved her poor discipline. But Alice wasn't one for listening. Belligerence ran in the Boucher family, alongside a propensity to blackmail people.

Ed drank tepid tea, took a bite from a smoked salmon and cream cheese sandwich, and returned to his crossword. His chest felt tighter than normal. He could hear his failing heart thumping erratically. A dodgy pump and a bloody pacemaker held him to ransom. A lesser man might have blamed his age, diet and alcohol intake and changed his lifestyle. Not him, real men didn't worry about their health.

Ed ordered himself to stay calm. He heard a woman's voice ask if the empty chair at his table was free. Ed shook his head, without shifting from his broadsheet. She ignored him. He heard the chair scrape as she plonked herself down. She made herself comfortable and spoke before he could protest.

'Oh gosh, it's Ed Boucher. What a coincidence!'

Ed glanced up into the sunlight shining through the glass roof. 'Sorry. Who are you?' he asked automatically, buying himself reaction time to prevent himself from yelling at her to stop stalking him.

'Samantha Sparrow. Rupert's daughter. I wanted a word with you.'

'Sorry about your father,' said Ed. Even though their families socialised in the same Hampshire circles, her intrusive behaviour annoyed him. Ed wasn't an elected politician or a celebrity, his privacy should be respected. 'I think we sent flowers. I am sure we did. Hope he had a good send-off. What brings you to Manchester?'

'Saturday's big fight. PR for the joint sponsors. Presenting a cheque to John Budd's family. Could I ask you a few questions about my father and Alice?'

'Fire away,' said Ed. Alarm bells rang, but he hoped he masked his fear.

'His diary said you saw him twice the week before he passed, and I was wondering … you and a girl called Kitty Elms on the same day. Is Kitty Alice?'

Ed admired Samantha's porcelain teeth, bronzed flesh and the light blue cashmere cardigan that showcased pear-shaped breasts. She was the same age as Ed's daughter would have been if Lucy hadn't been hit by a train. The coroner had recorded an open verdict, unable to decide if it was misadventure or suicide. 'Never heard of Kitty Elms. Your late father recommended a colleague for an honour, and I was arranging an in-person statement.'

'Can you tell me who?'

'Sadly not. Against the Official Secrets Act,' he said. 'Look out for future honours lists. See if you recognise any of your father's closest friends.' He was lying. He had disappeared a sex allegation for twenty-five thousand pounds. Rupert had thanked him for not reporting it to the police or selling the story to the media. A week later, Rupert was dead. Coincidence or not, Ed didn't care. If Rupert couldn't live with the shame, not his problem. His word against a dead man who admitted his guilt by signing a non-disclosure agreement.

'He knows so many people. I wouldn't know where to start,' said Samantha.

'Did he talk about any problems? Financial? Health? Love?'

'Nothing. He did purchase uncut diamonds before he died. There's no trace of them. I've spoken to everyone he saw between buying and dying … you and Kitty are the only leads left…,' said Samantha.

'I'm a dead end too,' Ed smiled, and felt Sparrow's bag of uncut diamonds rub against his wedding tackle. 'I'm definitely not allowed to accept wine, holidays, hospitality, and absolutely no diamonds.' In other circumstances, he might have asked her out for dinner, except he didn't want to share a table, or a bed, with her father's wretched ghost. 'Got to go now. Very sorry about Rupert.'

'One more thing,' said Samantha. She handed him a business card with her name, the PR business name, Believe, a Kensington address, contact details and a "refreshingly innovative thinkers" strapline. 'My client, Viktor Andreyev, is coming to Manchester. His company, Baltic Power, is sponsoring Saturday night's boxing. He wants to meet you this weekend.'

'I am very busy,' Ed said, 'You're doing great PR if you're stopping Baltic Power from being sanctioned by the USA and Europe. Well done.'

'We do our best. I'll cut the crap. I'm a blunt operator. Viktor wants your "sex-pest" list.'

'Sorry. I'm playing cricket with the Winchester College Old Boys' third team over the weekend,' Ed said. 'Besides, I don't have a "sex-pest" list. Wouldn't know what one looked like.'

'It's not really a request as such. Viktor always gets his way,' said Samantha.

'What are you trying to tell me?'

'Viktor doesn't take no for an answer.'

There was a good reason Ed only blackmailed rapists, paedophiles and perverts. He knew how they thought. He was one of them. Spies were off-limits. Why would you hack off Putin and his mates like this Viktor bloke after Alexander Litvinenko died on TV from radioactive Polonium-210 poisoning? 'I still don't understand.'

'Yes, you do,' said Samantha. 'You raise your eyebrows slightly when you lie and your neck blushes red. You can sell us your "sex-pest" list and make some cash, or we can do it another way. I'd hate you to have an accident. Or Alice.'

'Uncut diamonds?' asked Ed. 'You can make me a sparkling offer right now that I can't refuse. I'd imagine you've already got my mobile number.'

'I'm just a messenger. I'll have to come back to you. Ask Alice to call me too.'

'Why?'

'Rupert left her a private letter. I want to give it to her, but the lawyers say she needs to sign for it in person,' said Samantha.

Ed nodded at Samantha, stood up and left his half-eaten sandwich on the table. He had to stay cool and not panic. Who else knew he was a blackmailer? If it was an open secret, he was in big trouble. Equally worrying — why was a dead kiddy fiddler writing to Alice from beyond the grave unless they had a secret relationship? No chance. Alice would never cheat on him.

Two

Although Ed Boucher was a worried man, he strolled away from Samantha Sparrow determined not to look back. He tried to spot her co-conspirators, but the station was too busy to assess who, if anyone, was following him. He took his time window shopping and waited for Samantha to leave the cafe. She left a couple of minutes after him, walked out of the station by the rear entrance. She didn't appear to interact with anyone, sauntered through the throng like a catwalk model in Milan, Paris or New York. Ed went down the escalator, spotted Alice, winked as he passed. He nodded to the male toilets, headed towards them and stepped inside.

The tangy smell of stale urine mingled with disinfectant reminded him of boarding school and absentee parents. His folks had chased diplomatic careers at the expense of their children. Ed had tried to avoid the same mistakes but failed. Too little love versus too much. Achieving the right balance was next to impossible. He checked the cubicles, they were empty. He stepped inside one, and felt a nudge. He had company, he locked the door. They hugged, prolonged the embrace. Kissed on the lips. Wanted to get salacious. Sex calmed his nerves. Reluctantly, they broke their hold. Their eyes glistened, their lust mutual, although it wasn't always.

'Here,' she whispered. An envelope was thrust into Ed's hand. He put it inside his blazer pocket.

'Is the non-disclosure agreement there?' He whispered softly too, his voice, like hers, competing against the splatter of piss on metal urinals and gushing hand dryers.

'Yes. Why were you talking to Samantha Sparrow?' asked Alice.

'Pure coincidence. She is sponsoring the boxing in Manchester.' Nothing escaped her attention. He didn't tell her about Sparrow's request to get in touch. If Alice and Samantha became friends that would undermine their bond.

'No questions about Rupert's death?'

'No, why would she? He killed himself. Nothing to do with us.'

'You would tell me?' asked Alice. 'We were blackmailing the poor bugger. Where are you staying?'

'The Malmaison. Swinging Vogue suite.'

'Can I join you?'

'I thought you had a flat in the city,' said Ed.

'Not with you in it.'

'Doesn't matter where I'm staying. Tonight, you're sleeping in another country.'

'Why?'

'We're on a winning streak, but everyone's luck runs out eventually. We know Hampshire inside out, but Manchester might as well be the moon. We might be putting ourselves at risk,' said Ed, knowing there was no 'might' about it. He was knee-deep in the brown stuff and didn't want Alice joining him.

'The scam is a work of art,' said Alice.

'Listen to me. Train out of the city,' said Ed. 'Fly out on your real passport. Mainland Europe. France. Germany. Spain.'

'Why?'

'No time for questions. Change to the Victoria Morant ID when you fly to Thailand.'

'What about you?'

'I'll follow … shortly. Have you got my new ID?'

Alice unzipped a rucksack pocket and produced a plastic folder. She pulled out two Irish passports, two driving licences, a handful of credit cards and two envelopes thick with UK and European cash. She handed him his and replaced hers. 'What do we do with our real selves?' asked Alice.

A good question. Post-traumatic stress disorder could trigger depression, anxiety and early retirement. Or the two of them could simply vanish. 170,000 people went missing in the UK every year. The vast majority returned after a few days. A thousand or so didn't. They stayed disappeared until their bodies were found hanging from a tree, hidden in the undergrowth or washed up on the beach or a riverbank. 'Not our most immediate problem,' said Ed.

'Shall we? One for the flight?' Her hand gripped him and bashed against uncut diamonds.

'You'll shoot afterwards?' asked Ed.

'Soon as you have,' said Alice.

THREE

At two in the afternoon, Owen Chard booked into the Malmaison hotel reception. Said they were staying for three days but might leave early. Becky had wanted to bypass the city and head south. She said Manchester was morbid, encapsulated by the doom and gloom music of Joy Division, named after the sex-slave wing of a Nazi concentration camp. She said their lead singer had hung himself. Owen said it was just another city full of lonely men wanting to fuck.

They picked a double in preference to a twin, a nod to the marriage narrative, separate rooms an unnecessary expense. They unpacked their overnight bags without speaking and returned downstairs to identify married mugs. They sat near the reception, eyeballing the front desk and the hotel entrance. Excited tourists in the big city. Maintained their public image, him older with a beard, expensive teeth and dyed hair, her much younger, looking for adventure. She did rejected and dejected without needing to act. Easy, if you were permanently strung out, throwing up in the mornings. Given her state of mind, he was surprised they'd made it this far across the M62. Every sting was a bonus. When she went, he'd make sure his next cash cow chick was free from drug issues. He'd produce a questionnaire.

Occasionally, Owen put down his newspaper, got up and asked questions at the reception. Each time he returned, he gave Becky a name and an online identifying location or business. Although they had four potentials, they could do with a couple more. Most would go out with friends and work colleagues, only a few would stay in the hotel and be ripe for exploitation.

Becky spotted him first.

Navy blue blazer, white chinos, an old school tie, strutted around like a peacock. A suitcase in one hand and suit carrier bag slung across his shoulder. The newcomer registered at reception. Owen followed, asked about ordering a morning newspaper. Listened to Ed Boucher book dinner for one at seven. His room and expenses should be charged to the Cabinet Office. Owen fed the info back to Becky. She looked up Ed online and found him on LinkedIn. His profile revealed ex-army and currently a civil servant. Becky said it had not been updated for several years. He was not on Facebook or Twitter and hardly registered on the web. He was ideal prey. Ed walked over to the lift while Becky pulled down her beanie and drifted towards the reception desk, pretending to ask about her own dinner reservation as she double checked solo Ed's booking.

Owen watched his cold fish banter with the restaurant manager. She was there, but not there. Same as she was on the Humber Bridge when they first met. Friendly, funny and flirty, but a million miles away from betraying any real emotion. She was an elastic band, liable to snap anytime.

—

FOUR

Normally, Ed would be impressed by his third floor Swinging Vogue suite. Twice the size of a standard double, it was a kitsch celebration of the Swinging Sixties. Unpacking his clothes, Ed stacked them in a wardrobe next to a wooden bookcase. Framed black and white photographs of Twiggy, Shrimpton and Faithful caught his eye. Ed's wife, Irene, had been a looker once, until everything shrank and shrivelled, including her brain.

Alice would be boarding her flight now. Once she was out of the country, she was safe. His own security was not so healthy. Ed had promised powerful people his silence, but he was about to betray them and his country when, not if, he sold his "sex-pest" database to Putin's Baltic Power pal. According to Google, Viktor was a billionaire energy investor, a former electrician from Ukraine who kept a low profile. How much were the names of establishment perverts worth to men waging war on the west? He would find out soon enough when Viktor offered him a tax-free golden handshake.

Ed read the letter Alice had given him about John Budd. The kinky boomerang cock was inspired and the cheeky tattoos. He put the letter back in the envelope and placed it on the writing desk. He checked the non-disclosure agreement paperwork. The NDA was impressive, although worthless as a legal document. It would never stand up in court, but they all signed when he produced it at a blackmail gig. Shame his and Alice's efforts had been wasted.

Ed called the dementia home where Irene lived and told her he was settled in his hotel. He moaned that his room was cramped, and he would probably order a pizza via room service and then watch television. There were a couple of cooking programmes on TV they liked to watch. He had an early start tomorrow and wanted a good night's sleep. On that note, he closed the conversation and told her he loved her deeply and was already missing her. He promised to call again tomorrow, as he always did, not that she would ever remember. He would miss her when he started his new life with Alice in Asia.

He should have a kip, recharge the batteries. His chest still ached and there was an unpleasant taste in his mouth. But now Alice was away, Ed could play, let his hair down and unstress himself. Half an hour later, he was downstairs lecturing James the barman on how to pour gin and tonic in a wide glass with lots of ice and a twist of lime. James, new to the job, had worked in marketing and communications until Covid, a savage war in Eastern Europe and spiralling living costs made his skills a luxury bosses could easily afford to ignore.

'Can I have one of those, just like our gin expert has ordered?' An uninvited sex kitten sat herself down next to him and purred. 'Mind if I join you? My table's booked for seven and I always like an aperitif before dinner. I'm Becky.'

Ed smiled at her and said his name was Edward but she could call him Ed. He asked James to fix another of his very special gin and tonics. He was glad he'd come prepared — he had GHB and uncut diamonds in his blazer pocket. He knew how to win a girl over, a date rape drug and diamonds were a girl's best friends. They ensured she would be putty in his hands.

FIVE

Was Ed Boucher the one? Was Ed going to kill Becky and the unwanted foetus inside her, a parting gift from a Russian invader who had raped her in Bucha back home in Ukraine? Would Ed do what she had failed to do on the Humber Bridge when Owen stopped her jumping to her death? What did a murderer and rapist look like when he wasn't wearing a Russian uniform? Did he sport a wig, blazer and a military tie and speak in a posh English voice? Did he have a pencil-thin moustache? How did you know he was the one?

You didn't. You lived and died in hope.

Becky hadn't jumped into the Humber estuary. The Mifepristone and Misoprostol abortion pills were left untouched in her car, parked underground near the hotel. Ever since the bridge, Owen had been in her face, keeping her busy, not giving her termination time. But she was conscious she was close to the legal deadline to end unwanted pregnancies.

She looked at Ed, her murderer-in-waiting, and decided yes, he was the one. Ed suggested as he was dining alone and she was eating by herself, they could free up a table for other guests. A great idea, she said and asked why he was in Manchester. He said he was on business, a civil servant. Becky replied she was here for pleasure, a leisure break. She was a corporate financier working for an international bank and wrote books in her spare time and had a good reason to celebrate her hobby. Ed asked why and she went all coy, acted embarrassed. He misread her modesty, called her a tease. Becky apologised, said she was a bit shy, didn't normally chat up strangers. Ed said a glass of wine would help her relax, it always worked with him and he was a shy boy too. Becky said a bottle was a great idea, and explained she had signed a worldwide three-book deal with a major global publisher. Soon she would kiss the corporate world of finance goodbye and she hoped Ed wouldn't talk about base interest rates, the pros and cons of ISAs and the consequences of excessive quantitative easing. Ed asked her to name a book of hers he could buy. Becky said she wrote crime fiction under a pseudonym to protect her employer and could not reveal her writer's name. 'Otherwise, I'd have to kill you.'

'How?'

'I'll tell you when I come back from powdering my nose.' Becky paused by the toilets, out of sight, and watched Ed spike her champagne flute. His sleight of hand was barely noticeable, like he was cleaning the glass. He used a G&T straw to stir the drug into the bubbly. All Becky had to do was drink the spiked fizz and surrender to a psycho. Like she had done with the Russian rapist Andrei Orlov when she thought her sacrifice might save her husband Marko and his brother, Borden, and their cousin, Symon.

Boucher's drugs would render her death painless, no matter what Ed did to her. She would no longer suffer from the violent invasions of her country and herself. 'I'm coming Marko, coming home to you.'

Six

What did Ed know about this Becky woman? She was by herself, that was a big tick. She had no friends in Manchester, otherwise she would have been out with them, another tick. She had a foreign Eastern European accent. probably here illegally. This was Becky's unlucky night. The GHB in her champagne would soon knock her out. Then she was his, he could do what he wanted with the slut.

Becky walked back towards him, dressed in black, ready to be attacked. She sat down and crossed her legs. Her little black dress rode up to reveal no panties. It fitted the hooker narrative and lowered his exposure if she complained after he beat her up. Becky opened her clutch bag, lilac green lace knickers squeezed in. She applied lipstick and pouted provocatively. 'A toast,' said Ed.

'Wait,' said Becky. She kissed him full on the lips and grabbed both champagne glasses, then offered one to Ed as she sipped the other. The glass hadn't been cleaned properly, his had a slight salty soapy taste.

'To us,' said Ed. 'You were saying you'll have to kill me if I knew your writer's name.'

'Very true. I'd have to tie you to the bed, ride you cowgirl and smother you with a pillow,' replied Becky.

'I've got a great plot about a top civil servant blackmailing the establishment. Gets paid in uncut diamonds. His latest sting is for a quarter of a million pounds to protect the name of a crippled rapist hero cop. Based on a true story,' said Ed. The Budd blackmail scam was trashed, but he could still enjoy a few fringe benefits.

'Tell me more. My agent will be all gooey when I tell her about your sexy posh voice and your crime fiction idea. The way you speak makes me so horny,' said Becky.

'If you steal my blackmail story, you'll owe me commission,' said Ed.

'Cash or in kind?'

He loved her saucy arousal. 'Uncut diamonds.' He showed her the contents of a small drawstring black bag. 'Look at these beauties. Each one of them is worth several thousand pounds. Hold one. You only know they're valuable because I've told you. That's the beauty of them.'

'Shall we forget eating? Let's fuck. Do some coke. You've got a big dick and I need some holes filling,' said Becky.

Ed thought Becky was filthy perfect. What would knock the bitch out first? The drugs or his fists and feet?

SEVEN

One hand held a champagne bottle and two glass flutes and the other steadied Ed. Becky had incapacitated him too well. Ed wasn't capable of walking in a straight line, touching the tip of his nose, or killing her. The spiked drink had fucked him, not her.

In the lift upstairs, Becky propped Ed in the corner. She imagined the spirit of Marko by her side. He would have said if she let Ed kill her, others would die because she hadn't stopped him. When they had been asked a similar question about opposing the aggressors, they'd been unequivocal. They could have run when the Russians invaded, but they stayed and died in the hell that was Bucha.

She spoke under her breath in her naive language. 'Fuck you Ed Boucher, English rapist. Fuck you Andrei Orlov, Russian rapist. Fuck you Vladimir Putin, who raped a free country.' Becky could make at least one of them pay. If Boucher had raped and killed, she wanted names and details for the police.

She dragged Ed slowly from the lift to the entrance to the Swinging Vogue suite, propped him against the wall and opened the door. They entered, Ed was unsteady on his feet, his eyes struggled to focus. When he stumbled, his hands managed to take the brunt of the fall. 'What's happened?' Ed slurred.

'You're wrecked,' Becky replied. She helped him up from the floor, sat him on the four-poster bed and looked at him closely. Ed needed a pickup.

Becky produced a wrap from under her dress, took his wallet from his blazer and used his credit card to divide the powder into four lines. She rolled a brand new twenty into a tight tube. With her guidance, he snorted the coke. His eyes lit up. 'Ever been tied to a bed?'

'No.'

'I want to film us fucking,' said Becky. 'What's your password?' She wanted access to his digital world to find the evidence of rape and abuse. He gave it to her, too wasted to say no. Becky wrote the six-digit code on the mirror in the en suite and looked at her reflection. Andrei Orlov stared back at her, as he always did until she could focus on her own image and forget his. She had initially mistaken Owen for Orlov stepping out of the mist on the Humber Bridge when they had first bumped into each other, although she never told him. Half smashed herself, she needed to sober up fast. She stuck two fingers down her throat and heaved until her emptied stomach hurt.

Back in the bedroom, she stripped Ed naked and bound his wrists and ankles to the four-poster bed using his belt and her black nylon stockings. She placed her flick knife on the bedside table and noticed he had a pacemaker to calm down a dodgy ticker. Becky also noticed Samantha Sparrow's business card. She picked it up, inspected the wording and hoped SS wouldn't be knocking on the door and interrupting the party. 'Who is Samantha Sparrow?'

'She's Alice's nemesis.'

'Who is Alice?'

'My granddaughter.'

'Is Alice coming here tonight?'

'Sent her to Europe. Asia by the end of the week. Escaping.'

'Who from?'

'Nobody and everyone. Keep your eyes on the Sparrow.'

'Why?'

'Sparrow is demanding my "sex-pest" list for Putin and Andreyev. What a nightmare, money follows money.' He laughed. Spittle formed on his lips, snot ran out of his nose, sweat glistened on his forehead. His eyelids drooped.

'Don't go falling asleep on me. We've got a lot to talk about. You're a very nasty man. Or a complete fantasist making all this shit up,' said Becky. She slapped him hard across the face. 'Wake up, rapist. I want a full confession.'

EIGHT

The bell in the Piccadilly Tavern rang for last orders. TV screens broadcast looped boxing previews. Becky hadn't texted and Owen didn't have a clue what to do. Although they selected targets carefully, he knew they would eventually collide with a violent psychopath. Since they'd hooked up on the Humber, they had hit on a dozen lonely hearts who each reluctantly handed over two grand to avoid exposure as adulterers. All of them had to be physically encouraged to part with their money.

In Hull, Owen poked an Asian fashion entrepreneur in the chest and pushed him against the wall. When he complained, Owen reprised Billy Whyte's catchphrase and told him he was talking to the wrong man.

In York, Owen emulated Ben Kingsley in *Sexy Beast*, grabbed a tech development manager by the throat and spat in his face while he shouted the payment instructions.

In Harrogate, Owen held a software developer by the nuts like Gene Hackman did in *Mississippi Burning*. Owen used the same trick on a teacher in Newcastle, a trade union official in Sunderland, an engineer in South Shields and a dentist in Durham.

In Wakefield, Owen wrestled with a car dealer and ground his head into the en suite's tiled floor until blood overflowed like a blocked toilet.

In Leeds, a social worker was head butted. In Huddersfield, Owen eyeballed an advertising executive until he cried, half-inching a leaf out of Joe Frazier's intimidation book. Did the same to a management accountant in Bradford.

And in Halifax, Owen bog-washed a staff nurse when he refused to play ball. Another Billy Whyte white porcelain confession replay.

There was an alternative scenario. Addict Becky was the aggressor. High on drugs, hurting Ed. Owen raced across Piccadilly Gardens. He entered the hotel's crowded lobby packed with boxing fans and pushed his way through the scrum blocking his path to the lift. He pressed the lift button and waited, fearing the worst.

NINE

Becky started filming on Ed's mobile, held the camera in front of her face and introduced herself, using her real name, Angelina Kozar. Welcomed her guest to tonight's special one-off podcast. 'Hello, Ed. Great to see you tonight. Let's cut to the money shot. Would you have raped or killed me if I was all doped up instead of you?'

'I feel sick,' said Ed.

'That's the drugs talking. Were you going to rape me and then kill me and my unborn baby?'

'What…?'

'Why did you try to drug me?'

'I didn't,' he slurred. 'I don't feel well. My chest and arms hurt.'

'You're a liar. What's in this little container?' She held up a small bottle retrieved from his blazer pocket. 'Says GHB on the label. It's a date-rape drug, isn't it? Stay awake.'

'Call me a doctor, please,' begged Ed.

'What were you planning to do when I was unconscious?'

'Fuck you. We agreed to sex.'

'I've not consented. You're talking rape,' said Becky.

'I can't breathe.'

'Have you raped before?'

'Burning spiders are crawling over me. Brush them away. Please.'

'How many women have you raped?' asked Becky.

'You'd never understand. Please save me. I'll pay you.'

'What's the password to the locked videos?'

'My loving her saves lives,' said Ed.

He sounded like the Russian rapist, Andrei Orlov, justifying himself. She had to be sick again. When she returned, Boucher had fallen asleep, snot and spittle dried on his face. She decided she would give him five minutes respite and switched off the camera, airdropping the video to her own mobile. She checked his emails. Normal messages, nothing suspicious. She checked his diary. Two meetings tomorrow. Detective Inspector Nigel Watts and Chief Constable Sir Richard Hurst. On Friday, Jane Church, the editor of the local newspaper, and John Budd's neurosurgeon, Helen Tapody. Becky opened the John Budd file. A one-page summary outlined Budd's bravery; an abuse letter undermined his heroism. Was his reputation worth a quarter of a million pounds? Boucher's mobile rang, she answered instinctively. 'Hello.'

'Is Ed there?'

'No, he's tied up at the moment. Who is calling?' Becky leaned over to her clutch bag, took out her lilac green lace knickers and stuffed them in Ed's mouth. Becky didn't want him interrupting their conversation.

'Samantha. Samantha Sparrow. Is that you Alice?'

'Yes,' Becky lied.

'I've been dying to speak to you. Did Ed tell you? My late father wrote you a letter. I've got it with me.'

'That's nice of him,' said Becky.

'Why would he write to you?'

'I'll read the letter and tell you.'

'When can I give it to you?' asked Samantha.

'Where are you?' asked Becky.

'The Dakota hotel in Manchester. Pop around. Presidential suite. A Baltic Power booking.'

'Call me first thing tomorrow, I'm shagged,' said Becky, and gave Samantha her number.

'OK Alice. See you soon,' said Samantha. 'Good news. Viktor has a sparkling uncut stone offer for Ed. Ask him to call me ASAP.'

Becky cut the conversation and wrote Sparrow's number on the en suite mirror, then photographed the mirror and wiped it clean with a small wet towel. She went back into the suite and checked on Ed tied to the bed.

His lips were blue, the bugger was dying on her.

She went into automatic emergency nurse mode. Removed his knicker gag, felt for a pulse on his left wrist. Checked his neck and then straddled Ed. Placed the heel of her hand on the centre of his chest. Put the palm of one hand on top of the other, interlocked her fingers. Leaned forward and used her body weight to compress his chest and start CPR. Next, she tilted Ed's head, lifted his chin, pinched his nose, sealed his mouth and blew into his lungs and watched his chest rise. 'Don't you die on me, you selfish bastard. You haven't confessed yet. How dare you escape justice?'

TEN

Ed Boucher wasn't scared. He thought he would be but he wasn't. He could see his future. There wasn't one. His body was wrecked, his mind as clear as a polished diamond. He knew, one way or another, his time was up. She had a knife. Saw her put it by the bed. Tomorrow he would remember nothing. Not that it mattered. He wouldn't be here. At first, he thought she was going to use the blade on him. If, like Alice, she knew how to wield the cold steel, she would probably slice clean through one of his main arteries. Instant loss of consciousness. Death in a matter of seconds. A quick transition from life to no life. If she was an amateur who carried the blade for show, his demise would be slower and messier.

Whatever she did, he was well anaesthetised by the booze and the GHB.

He understood what she had done. She had switched the drinks and he'd been too excited to notice. Dropped his guard because the pretence was over. A rebirth with Alice in Asia was his last chance of happiness.

The bitch was clever. Posed as a fuck buddy pick-up. Tied him to the bed. Used his own belt. Fed him coke. An opportunity not to be sniffed at. He'd bragged about blackmailing John Budd's healthcare fund for a quarter of a million pounds to impress her, because she claimed she was a famous author. He would have asked the top cop for a tenth of that. Far more realistic. Not that she was interested. All she had wanted to do was ask silly questions about rape.

What did it matter to her?

Two consenting adults could do what they liked, as long as children weren't hurt. Besides, how did you define a child or consent? When a woman or a child said no, they really meant yes. Playing hard to get was all part of the thrill, the chase. Men hunted. Women and kids were their natural prey, seed recipients.

If he didn't die by the blade, maybe the burning spiders the size of crabs crawling over his body would kill him. They would burn his flesh. Eat him alive. Legs like claws, cutting and slashing him to ribbons. Would the police find him tied to the bed? A bloody unidentifiable meaty mess? They'd have to use DNA or dental records to name him. A kinky death guaranteed media exposure. The perverted civil servant mired in corruption. Would they find out about the family's secrets? Only Alice was left to spill the beans. Lucy had caught the wrong train home. Cancer had cancelled the memoirs of his diplomatic parents, Lord Alfred and Lady Edith. Dementia separated Irene from reality, the Lamb-Percy family trust's old money controlled by her brothers. He could never access the cash because they never trusted him. That's why he blackmailed bastards like them. Made them pay for ostracising him. Boarding school, the army, the civil service. Nobody ever appreciated his talents. Only Lucy and Alice understood him. Nothing to do with money or sex. Purely raw stress relief. Not that it mattered.

Chronic heart disease coupled with excessive intoxication had brought his innings to a premature close. He wouldn't be opening for the College Old Boys at the weekend. Nor would he be sailing anymore, eyeballing from behind dark glasses the long legs and short shorts of the sailing club's teens.

Ed wanted to beg Becky to let him go. Except he'd lost the ability to speak. He couldn't move a muscle. His limbs didn't work. Everything hurt. His chest. His jaw, neck, back and tummy. He felt sick. The classic signs of a heart attack? They had warned him many times, but he'd ignored them. Truth be told, he'd rather pop his clogs suddenly, taken by surprise.

In death, would Lucy be waiting for him alongside his parents? Would he finally find out what happened on that station platform?

No chance.

Ed didn't believe in God or an afterlife. You were alive. Then you weren't. He knew there would only be a void. Had Alice pushed Lucy in front of the train? Only two people possibly knew for sure. Lucy was dead. Did Alice remember? Was that why she self-harmed and willingly let him use and abuse her every which way? It drove Irene nuts that she never knew for sure if Alice had killed Lucy. To be honest, the uncertainty had caused him untold undiagnosed damage. Not that it mattered. It's all over now. Stay Alice. Stay free, even if you're without me.

Cut.

ELEVEN

A middle-aged drunken Romeo and Juliet crowded Owen's space in the foyer of the Malmaison hotel. When the lift arrived, the drunk barged past, pulled inebriated Juliet towards him and groped her backside. Unimpressed, Owen asked what floor they wanted. The couple, oblivious, leaned on the buttons and stopped the lift doors from closing. Romeo peered over Juliet's shoulder and winked salaciously, mouthed 'third floor' and resumed swapping spit. 'Want to join us for a threesome? My mate fancies you,' said Romeo in a German accent.

'You're talking to the wrong man,' replied Owen. He grabbed Juliet and threw her out of the lift. Did the same with Romeo, butted his head and drew blood. A guest stepped between them as the drunken German swung at thin air. 'What floor?'

'Three,' said the guest.

'Me too.'

When they reached their destination, they both stepped out. Owen pretended to text and moved slowly towards the Swinging Vogue suite. The door should be ajar for ease of access. In the silence, Owen heard heavy breathing. A couple shagging? His fellow lift companion cocked an ear to the energetic love making, checked the room names and walked away down the corridor.

Owen opened his mobile camera to record hardcore sex. Hard to deny an illicit affair when your cock was inside a woman who wasn't your wife. He entered and noticed a strong smell of sick. A screen hid the bed from his view. He walked past the screen and looked left. A naked Ed Boucher was spreadeagled on the bed with Becky riding him cowgirl, both oblivious to Owen's entrance. 'What the hell are you doing with my wife, you bastard?' They ignored him. Owen said it louder. 'Stop fucking my wife!' Still no response. Owen was unsure what to do. Did he start demanding money or join in? Except they weren't shagging. Underneath Becky's bare bottom Boucher's dick was limp, her hands were pressing down on his chest. She was counting to herself. Owen put his arms around her shoulders and wrestled with her briefly to untangle her from Boucher's torso. 'What's going on?'

'He's dead.'

Owen felt for a pulse. There was none. Owen reached for the beside phone to call reception for an ambulance and stopped. Boucher, bound to the bed, was not a good look. Becky's DNA was all over the dead man. They would arrest her. She could claim it was an accident, but why would anyone believe her? Owen was in the clear — he wasn't in the room when Boucher died. Plenty of witnesses saw him in the Japanese restaurant, in the pub and scuffling with the German couple in the lift. He'd be on CCTV.

He toyed with mitigation scenarios, but there were none. How was Becky going to explain the delay? He looked at Ed Boucher's dead body. Would she drop him in it when the filth interrogated her? Forced her to cold turkey until she gave them what they wanted? 'What are you going to tell the police?'

'The truth. He was a rapist who tried to drug me. It would be me lying there if I hadn't switched the glasses.'

Would that wash with the cops? Did it sound plausible enough? Except didn't she just say the drugs were in his body, not hers? That would undermine her narrative. They had to run. 'Go and clean yourself up. I'll untie him. We're going to walk away. Anyone ever asks, he was alive when you left the room. You blew him to thank him for dinner. OK?'

'Why the graphic detail?'

'The cops will be distracted by the salacious detail,' replied Owen. Better to be branded a slut than a murderer. Owen untied the nylon bindings and handed her the black stockings. She took them and went into the bathroom. He undid the belt and put it on the back of the chair nearest the writing desk. There was a file with the name JOHN BUDD on the front. The name was familiar, although he couldn't place it. There was also a black bag. He looked inside and saw half a dozen stones the size of Kola cubes. He put them back and turned to Ed. Rolled the dead man's body in the bed onto its side. Rested the head on a pillow, tried to make it look natural.

The hotel cleaning staff would find Boucher tomorrow or the next day. By then they'd be in Liverpool, Chester, Birmingham, or even further down south. Perhaps they should go their separate ways. It would be easy enough to convince her to end the partnership, her heart wasn't in it anyway. Owen and Becky had worked for six weeks and earned thirty grand between them. Eight went on expenses, the rest was profit. Better than PAYE, better than acting, far better than writing. Even successful Hollywood writers had to survive on peanuts.

He picked up Ed's clothes and hung them up in the wardrobe. Inspected Ed's wallet. Flipped it open. There was a civil service ID card. Family photographs of Ed with attractive women, presumably his wife and daughter. Credit cards. Driver's licence. Details about his pacemaker in case of an emergency.

Too late. Ed had already checked out.

Inside the wardrobe, various documents were hidden under Ed's collection of wigs. An Irish passport. A driver's licence for a Seamus Morant. A large open envelope with two thick cash wedges — one Sterling, the other Euros.

A false passport meant Ed was either a criminal or a spy. Owen didn't care. He was only interested in self-preservation. Take the money and run. He'd read Cormac McCarthy's *No Country for Old Men* and would have loved to have played Chirugh if his agent Charlie Wolff had been influential enough to get him an audition with the Coen brothers. He'd shouted silently at the screen for Moss not to take water to the half-dead drug dealer. And had done the same when Moss had the chance to kill Chirugh. 'Shoot first, talk later while you're still alive'. Procrastination gets you killed. He pocketed the envelope with the cash, the passport and the driving licence.

Becky came out of the bathroom, glanced around the room and walked to the bedside table. She picked up incriminating evidence: Boucher's phone, Samantha Sparrow's business card, the knife, empty coke wraps and a half full GHB bottle. 'Let's go to our room. You take the lift. I'll take the stairs. Pack and discuss our next steps,' said Owen.

Becky glanced around the room again. He followed her gaze. The Scrabble bag with the Kola Cubes. She went over to the desk. Paused over the bag. 'He's bent, like us. A blackmailer,' said Becky.

'What do you mean, a blackmailer like us?'

She told him about Boucher's scam.

Once she had finished, Owen pictured himself swapping identities with the dead man. A quarter of a million quid would change Owen's life. He had never eaten off silver spoons. His family was blue collar dead, worked and played and drank and smoked themselves into early-bird cremations, an unhealthy combination of excessive boozing and shit genetics that would be his inheritance.

His imagination was running riot, and he knew he was fooling himself by thinking about stealing another man's identity. Pure fantasy, like he would play around with script ideas for ages, searching for that eureka moment. *Hanging Around*, his live TV execution thriller, was the big game changer, until the most influential Scottish literary and TV agent turned it down and drove him despondently to the Humber.

But he could pull this off. He could play Ed Boucher and ask the top cop for the diamonds. Did they know each other? An anonymous civil servant from London and a high-profile northern police chief?

Unlikely.

But what about Boucher's dead body? They could swap. He could reciprocate. Lend Ed his name. He could borrow the Seamus Morant alias for a short while. Spend a few weeks overseas. Leave the uncut diamonds in a safe deposit box in England. Return and resurrect Owen Chard. Claim he'd gone to find himself on an offline bothy tour of the Scottish Highlands. The establishment would cover everything up to protect its own.

The idea was so preposterous it might work.

But he needed Becky's help to explain away a dead body. Would she be interested? There was one way to find out, ask. 'Do you think I look like Ed?'

Becky stared at him, appeared to give his question serious thought. It showed they were still on the same wavelength. 'Perhaps.'

Owen was doing some considering too. Same weight. Same height. Same build. A haircut and a clean shave for himself and Ed. He could do posh. Speak posh. Walk posh. Act posh, like one of the establishment's elite who expected the waves to part when they walked among the plebs. 'Are there details of his meetings on his phone?'

'Yes.' said Becky.

'Are you up for it, Mrs Chard?'

TWELVE

Are you up for it? Owen, forever the opportunist, had the same semi-serious intensity he'd had on the Humber Bridge. 'We've got ten minutes to decide,' he said. 'Shall I explain?'

'Go ahead,' she replied. 'What's on your mind?'

'Owen Chard dies tonight, and I become Ed Boucher.'

Becky was right on the bridge when she called him a real comedian. He was a very funny man, not. 'How does that happen?'

'You call reception. Tell them your husband is dead. I impersonate Ed. Collect the cash. Claim an administrative error at a later date. I am resurrected. A richer man in a poor man's world.'

'You're crazy,' said Becky. 'What about Boucher's family? They'll never have closure.'

'You're talking to the wrong man. No sympathy for rapists. We need to cut my hair, shave my beard off, give me an Errol Flynn moustache. And you need to ditch the hooker outfit.'

'We can't put a beard and hair on Ed?'

'Doesn't matter. Nobody noticed me in the hotel. I'm a nobody.'

Half an hour later, Owen was Ed Boucher in the Swinging Vogue suite. 'Are you ready?' she asked.

'Sure. After this, we don't want any sympathy for Owen.' He slapped her face twice. 'Sorry, got to keep it real.'

Crying, Becky called reception. Said her husband had a fatal heart attack. They'd had an argument in a friend's room, left to let him cool off and found him dead when they returned.

Within minutes, the duty manager and two security staff arrived to help her and her friend Ed Boucher with her bereavement. Two police constables attended after the hotel reported an unresponsive man in a room, both too young to remember prime-time Owen Chard, now a bald corpse.

Forty-five minutes later Norma Jones, the on-call emergency doctor, confirmed Owen Chard was dead. The doctor spotted the pacemaker and told the police there was nothing suspicious to report about the man pronounced dead at the scene. She said there might be an autopsy as it was a sudden death and the deceased had been drinking, but that was the coroner's decision in his or her good time.

The police officers asked if Becky was able to formally identify Owen's body and could they put her down at the next of kin? She nodded and said she was a refugee from the Ukraine and her real name was Angelina Kozar. Becky Letts was a pseudonym to help her find work in England as an actress. Owen was mentoring her before their friendship evolved into love and marriage. She had missed her last two periods and was having his baby. She stroked the slight bulge above her abdomen. Norma noticed the fresh bruising on Becky's cheeks. Becky said she banged her head on the sink when she threw up after finding her husband unresponsive in the bed. Norma asked if Becky had a headache, felt dizzy or nauseous, and instructed her to follow her finger movements with both eyes. Although satisfied there was no concussion, Norma was worried about the health of her baby. Any abnormal pains, Becky should go straight to A&E. Was she attending antenatal clinics?

Becky lied and said she was.

After the doctor and the police departed, Michael Myles, the hotel general manager arrived with a local undertaker to remove the deceased. He asked Becky if she wanted the hotel to notify Owen's family and friends on her behalf. Becky replied that it was all OK, she was the next of kin as his wife. She had help on hand. Ed was a close friend who had sponsored her in the UK after the Russian invasion. They hooked up by chance when they bumped into each other in the lift. She said she would wait until the body was removed before she made the call to Owen's family in Ottawa, Canada. They were five hours behind UK time. Until then, Becky asked everyone in the room to promise not to leak the death of the actor who had once played Billy Whyte in *Northern Filth* on social media until she had spoken to them.

Thirteen

Contrary to popular critical opinion, Owen had taken his acting seriously. Smart arse TV reviewers claimed Billy Whyte was merely Owen Chard playing himself, but they were wrong. He had worked hard developing the character and refused to accept the cheap cliché that soap actors couldn't act. Owen was professional at the start. Always learned his lines and turned up on time early doors. Always sober, before Billy took off and everything went to shit. As Owen's ego and the money spiralled, he could no longer distinguish between himself and the character. If only he had died in his twenties. He'd be in good company: Heath Ledger, Kurt Cobain, Janis Joplin, Amy Winehouse, River Phoenix, Jim Morrison, James Dean, Jimi Hendrix, Brian Jones and Ronnie Van Zant. His fame, or infamy, would have been assured. There would have been no slow decline into rusty ordinariness once his creative spark had been extinguished and he had to buy his own booze and drugs again.

Owen knew he had to be cruel to be kind, at least in the short run. The time gap worked in his favour. They rehearsed calls to his ex-wife, Caroline, and his agent, Charles. It took them an hour to get it right. He said her pregnancy was inspired and would take the wind out of Caroline's self-righteous sails. As Becky was about to leave the room, Owen stopped her.

'Thanks for doing this, Becky, or should I call you Angelina?' asked Owen.

'Either. As long as there's no more honey-trapping,' said Becky.

'You're free as a bird.'

'One favour in return. My pregnancy is real.'

'You're not carrying a baby inside you? You've been drinking and smoking and sniffing ever since we met.'

'I was meant to be dead. I've got pills in the car. I'll get them. We can do the termination after my confession.'

Owen coughed and cleared his throat. 'What are you going to confess?'

'Not us being petty criminals. What happened to me in Ukraine. You don't want to hear that, you won't sleep. I need someone with me when I terminate my pregnancy and there is only you in Manchester.'

Only him? He was an actor, a writer, a storytelling social anecdotalist who enjoyed beer and the pub and banter with his mates. He was a drinker and an occasional smoker. Now he was a real-life terminator, not a role he ever envisioned playing. He wasn't even sure he agreed with abortions.

FOURTEEN

Alone in his room on the fourth floor, Owen read and reread the contents of the John Budd folder and thoroughly familiarised himself with the brain-damaged police officer. Pretending he had to learn a script for an audition in the morning, he read the allegation letter several times. Laughed at the kinky boomerang cock. Good detail, ditto the tats if they were accurate, dumb if they weren't.

He thought about his devastated girls four thousand miles away. His two teenage daughters, Sophia and Victoria, innocents in his numerous battles with his ex-wife, Caroline. He wanted to call and confess it was all a practical joke but forced himself to focus on the stark reality of the situation. Caroline never gave a damn about him. Turned the girls against him with stories that became exaggerated tabloid fact. She never told anyone she was as big a hedonist as him when they were making it as rock stars. Nor did she say she developed the serious drug habit he had avoided. And he never told anyone she inspired his biggest hit record.

Truth be told, she deserved a telling.

Owen toyed with the Kola cubes in the black bag and shook them like they were Mahjong dice. What were the five stones worth? He counted the money stolen from the Swinging Vogue. Five grand sterling and six grand in Euros.

He felt bad. Not about the cash, people ripped each other off all the time. He felt guilty about leaving Becky on her lonesome. Perhaps they should have stayed together tonight. She shouldn't be alone after seeing a human die in front of her eyes. That must spook you, play on your mind when you tried to sleep. Perhaps he should have been in the room when she made the calls. Telling a stranger a loved one had died wasn't easy either. Then again, surviving a war was pretty shit too. He didn't understand why Putin had invaded a neighbour without provocation. Maybe Putin thought the Ukrainian people would roll over like they did when Russia stole the Crimea a decade ago. Putin got a bloody surprise when they fought back. Thought it would take a week to seize the country, but the Russian dictator miscalculated the mood of ordinary people. Ukrainians were different. They put national pride before profit. Unlike him. Money mattered more than anything when you didn't have it anymore.

FIFTEEN

Two in the morning in Manchester, a thousand miles from home. Time to start the Becky Letts death dance. In the en suite, Becky burned her fake passport and washed the debris down the sink. That felt good. Goodbye Becky, hello Angelina. She called Caroline on Owen's mobile. It was nine in the evening in Ottawa, five hours behind Manchester time. A voice answered thousands of miles away but sounded like next door. 'Is that Caroline Chard?'

'Yes. Who are you?'

'My name is Angelina. I am Owen's wife.'

'Typical. He kept that quiet. Why are you calling on his mobile? Is he OK?' asked Caroline.

'No, he's not. He died suddenly tonight, a suspected heart attack in a hotel.'

'Jesus, that's terrible.'

'I was with him. He didn't pass alone. We were in Manchester. He was trying to place a script.'

'Still chasing the impossible dream,' said Caroline. 'Why couldn't he have been a management accountant or a solicitor?'

'Seemed happy enough to me,' said Angelina.

'We'll be over in two or three days to help with the funeral and his estate. Soon as we can organise flights,' said Caroline.

'About that. Owen didn't want you involved in his funeral. There's nothing in his will for you or the girls. No offence, but he was very bitter about how you treated him. Said you were the inspiration for Sorry, I Made You Cry When I Almost Died and has the deathbed pics to prove it. I believe your girls have never seen them. Stay away from me and the media or I'll publish them for the world to see,' said Angelina, and listened to Caroline's tears as her daughters tried to calm their mother.

Next, she woke Charlie Wolff and dived into Owen's script without pausing for breath. 'Hi, I am Owen Chard's new wife. My name is Angelina Kozar. I am a Ukrainian film and TV agent. Before he died last night, he appointed me to exclusively act for him.'

'Died?'

Angelina explained. Charles listened. Everything was under control in Manchester. Angelina had identified the body for the police and would handle any media enquiries.

'He's sacked me?'

'I have. Owen said you didn't have the skills or the contacts to build on his Billy Whyte work. He used to curse you night and day. I was helping him rebuild his career. Any media, you pass onto me or I'll be telling them a few stories about you.'

The conversation ended as abruptly as it had done with Caroline. Angelina threw up. That was horrible. A WhatsApp message interrupted her shame. Encrypted from the world. Three mobiles on the bed beside her. It was Ed's. A message from an Alice. 'Are you OK? I missed my flight.'

Angelina scanned the historical messages between Alice to Ed to emulate their chatty tone. 'Fine. Hope you catch the next one. Sleeping. Nighty night.'

Lying in bed, Angelina was exhausted, but sleep wouldn't come. The seconds ticked like minutes. She was in a basement. Then she wasn't. She was in a classroom. Then she wasn't. She was running. Then she wasn't. She was on a bridge. Then she wasn't.

Then she was here.

She got out of bed and checked her watch. It was four in the morning. Put on her jeans and boots. The *CUTE BUT 101% PSYCHO* tee. She used the flick knife to slash and shred the little black cocktail dress, the stockings, the high heels and the lilac green lace knickers and then put them all in a pillowcase.

She walked through the empty hotel and stepped out into twenty-four-hour city centre Manchester. The streets were alive with noisy drunks and minimum wage shift workers cleaning up their mess. She looked up and down the length of Piccadilly and saw people camped out in doorways, huddled against walls. The drunks and the homeless living it large in the cold concrete city.

Across the road, a rough sleeper was curled into a ball. She walked right and crossed the A6. Didn't want to scare them. Bad enough to be sleeping rough in a rich nation like the UK.

She headed down Ducie Street, turned right into Dale Street and looked for a large industrial bin to ditch the slashed honey-trapping gear. She found a half-full bin next to the headquarters of Boohoo and emptied the contents. Ripped clothes wouldn't look out of place in a waste bin next to a fast-fashion business. She pushed half a dozen coke wraps and the empty GHB bottle deep into the bin, safe from casual bin surfers. The knife was too dangerous to leave lying around so she ditched it in a drain. The rain would wash it down the sewer, where all weapons belonged.

Satisfied, she walked down Paton Street and found an all-night convenience store. Bought BLT and egg and bacon sandwiches, two chocolate croissants, two bottles of water, two cans of Coke, toothpaste, soap, wipes, tissues, chocolate digestive biscuits, a giant bar of milk chocolate and four packs of sanitary towels for the termination.

She walked into the car park at the back of the hotel and located her borrowed VW Golf in the underground basement. She opened the boot, took out a rucksack containing a pair of spare jeans, tops and underwear. Angelina had travelled light with Owen and had never thought about clothes when she was ready to top herself, because there were no best dressed suicide awards in heaven or hell. The rest of her stuff was still at Jason and Jessica's house in Whitefield, including her real passport and her Ukrainian mobile. The English couple had been her host family when she arrived homeless in England.

She took off the *CUTE* tee and put on an ordinary white one. Checked under the seats for anything that belonged to her. The car was clean apart from receipts. They were Owen's responsibility, not hers. The glove compartment contained Jessica's 'kill-a-life' pack. Jessica had arranged for an abortion kit after an ultrasound scan confirmed Angelina was pregnant. Angelina locked the car, retraced her footsteps and tiptoed up to the homeless sleeper. She placed the plastic shopping bag packed with food next to him or her and kept the sanitary towels under her arm.

She crossed the road to her hotel and stopped short of the kerb as a group of runners silently jogged towards her. At the front of the pack was the heavyweight boxing champion of the world, Wolfgang Muller. She hated him. Wolfgang's social media feeds pictured him with Putin and the bloke who headed the Wagner group. She stepped into the big man's path, shouted in her native language. 'Glory to Ukraine. Glory to the Heroes.' The front runners sidestepped her to avoid a collision, two of the runners behind Muller flipped her the middle finger and one at the back swivelled around and gave her a thumbs up. He shaped his hand in the iconic three-fingered trident that symbolised Ukrainian statehood and blew her a kiss and carried on running. She hoped Marko was watching from above. He'd be pleased she had cleansed herself. Spiritually, mentally and physically. RIP fictitious, unloved, lonely Becky Letts. Welcome back Angelina Kozar. Warrior not worrier.

SIXTEEN

Across the road from the hotel, Alice stamped out a cigarette and nursed the takeaway coffee. The mobile message revealed nothing beyond Ed was awake. She had pretended she was homeless, even though she had a flat in Fallowfield, the city's student quarter near Manchester University.

A group of half a dozen men approached. A couple of them asked for casual sex, handjobs in return for two half-empty beer bottles, a 'buy one get one free' offer that was impossible to resist.

Alice said yes, if they didn't mind her blood dripping on their cocks. She held out both hands streaked with wet blood. Said she would do them both at the same time. They could all enjoy licking off a pink semen cocktail from her hands after they'd both ejaculated.

As they walked quickly away, Alice laughed and forgot all about them, children masquerading as grown-ups, acting out their porn-world fantasies. She had disobeyed Ed, openly defied his instructions and not flown out of the country. He'd taken it well, too well, when she messaged about missing her connection.

She reviewed her situation.

Earlier, an undertaker's ambulance parked outside the hotel. Two men in suits opened the back of the vehicle and took out a trolley. Ten minutes after they arrived, they exited the hotel. Their trolley, heavier with a stiff on board, was loaded into the ambulance. Within sixty seconds they were gone, and the lights were off in the Swinging Vogue suite. Lights in two rooms on floors three and four came on. Alice had gone into the hotel and asked the night porter about spare rooms, chewed inconsequential nightshift fat. The porter said Owen Chard, the actor who played Billy Whyte in *Northern Filth*, had died of a heart attack, a middle-aged bald man kicked the bucket alone. She sent a text to Ed. By the time she returned to her homeless pitch, Ed had replied and created a nagging doubt in her head.

She googled Owen Chard and read first about his short pop career as Vic Savage, leader of new-wave-punk pioneers, Savaged by Sheep. They had two top ten singles. *Flat Earth*, about Luddites who refused to acknowledge obvious facts, such as the world was round, and *Sorry, I Made You Cry When I Almost Died*, an ode to drug overdoses and the pain endured by loved ones. Fed up with music once the hits dried up, Owen hung up his guitar and flattened his mohican. His teenage thug in *Prime Suspect* led to roles in *Rio*, *Kiss of Death* and *Wild West Boys*. For ten years he was Billy Whyte three times a week in *Northern Filth*. Film credits included *Rough House*, *Cannon Fodder*, *The Last Hooligan*, *Stalker* and *Tomorrow Belongs to Today*. His most recent film was an unsubtle Scottish remake of *Get Carter* called *Jimmy Jinx*. He'd played a sleazy chauffeur killed in the last act, falling from Arthur's Seat with a quart of whisky swilling in his guts. Owen had been busy for most of his acting career, although the credits vanished when Covid 19 stopped the world. He had two daughters. His wife, Caroline, had alleged he was violent towards her. There was lots of gossip about alleged flings with models and film actresses when he was Billy Whyte. He looked OK in his prime. There were no images of the current older, more mature model. This year, according to Wikipedia, he was focused on writing. Not any longer. The poor bastard was dead. Was he the angry head-butting man with a beard she saw in the lift getting off on the third floor? She downloaded a prime-time clean shaven Billy Whyte pic and couldn't tell. She searched You Tube for Savaged by Sheep videos and laughed at them. They were funny. Owen could sing about truth and overdoses and make it feel real. Shame he'd kicked the bucket. She would have liked to talk about his approach to creativity.

She parked Owen. He was dead. No longer relevant to her life beyond likes on social media. Alice was more intrigued about Ed's change of heart. One minute excited about blackmailing the kinky cock cop, the next demanding Alice flees England on the next available European flight. Alice had arrived early at Manchester's Piccadilly train station to make sure was Ed wasn't exposed to imminent danger. She replayed the Piccadilly station meeting between Ed and Samantha. Like Ed said, at first glance it might have been a pure coincidence. An accidental meeting. But Samantha had many reasons for a showdown with Ed. Had she revealed she was Alice's secret half-sister? Or was she questioning Ed about her father's death or telling him she knew about his fondness for young flesh?

After Sparrow had finished talking with Ed, Alice had followed her. Samantha had exited from the station's back entrance. An expensive black Range Rover with tinted black windows collected her. A giant got out of the car and opened the door for Samantha. The same man who'd exited from the front entrance of a Kensington town house seconds after Rupert had fallen head-first from the fourth floor, his brains oozing slowly from his smashed skull onto the pavement. Alice had tried to push them back into her father's head, but he was already well gone. Were they planning for Ed and her to have similar accidents? Was that why Ed wanted her to leave so quickly?

Thursday 9th June 2022
Seventeen

Angelina arrived in the breakfast room at eight. She sat facing the door, back to the wall. Ordered coffee and toast, and surfed the internet on the mobile her English host family, Jason and Jessica, had bought for her. Owen's death hadn't been announced on the news outlets, but there were rumours flashing up on Twitter and Facebook when she searched the actor's name. He wasn't popular enough to go viral. Owen entered the room and headed in her direction. He sat down at her table and made himself comfortable. He'd captured the dead man's cocky gait and aloof arrogance. She avoided looking at the wig on his head. She wanted to laugh at how ridiculous he looked compared to the hip-creative actor-writer persona he had carefully cultivated. She was wise to his vanity.

A middle-aged peroxided waitress asked if he wanted coffee or tea. Before he could reply, the waitress said quietly that she was sorry for their loss. She'd really liked Billy Whyte in *Northern Filth*. He was her favourite character. Reminded her of Spencer, her late brother until the drugs and drink claimed him. He'd fallen asleep outside in the middle of winter and woken up with severe frostbite. It cost him his legs, but not his addiction. Owen offered his condolences, and she blushed and touched his arm affectionately. A different waitress, same age, different hair, size and skin colour, brought coffee and toast and bowed in sympathy. They had a similar conversation. Her former husband was a squaddie, a no-nonsense fella like Billy. A third young foreign waitress with a Down Under accent took their order and said nothing; too young to remember Billy Whyte.

They ate in silence, staying in character in front of an unknowing audience. He had a full English and she went Continental, like she would have done back home. He asked how Owen's ex-wife and agent had taken the sad news.

'Badly.' Angelina said plans for a burial had been replaced by a quick, private cremation. Owen asked what she was going to do today while he pitched to the police chief. She said she would visit a friend to discuss her return home post-termination. Nina Mazur ran a refugee centre in the city centre, resettling and repatriating Ukrainians. She was a saint who smoked a pack a day to cope with the stress. Angelina handed him Boucher's phone with the ambiguous rape confession video on it. A copy was stored in her cloud. She gave Owen Ed's six-number code.

'Have you got Owen's mobile?'

'Yes.'

'Any messages?'

'A few people asking if the rumours are true.'

'Did you reply?'

'No.'

'Good. I might just pull this off,' said Owen. Angelina didn't tell Owen about the telephone call with Samantha Sparrow and her pretending to be Alice. He had enough on his plate without her adding more crap.

Eighteen

Alice hated lies more than anything else in the world. When she was famous as a writer or an artist doing a media Q&A, she would tell her interviewer she disliked disingenuous people who never said what they meant. There should be no secrets between friends, families and lovers, but inevitably there were. She was just as guilty as everyone else, hiding things from Ed, terrified of his reaction.

She woke at six. Too early to wake her grandfather. A do-gooder had left her a bagful of shopping. Alice looked inside. How kind and how pointless. How about a roof and a job? Alice was annoyed at sleeping so heavily that somebody had crept up on her. She took the bag and left it for another homeless person sleeping fifty yards from her.

She went for a walk around Manchester's city centre to clear her head and decide what to do next. She'd told Ed that she missed her flight, and his answer had been out of character. He hadn't rebuked her. In the toilet, he had stressed the urgency of getting out of the country and going to Thailand under the false ID. His reply was too chilled. 'Hope you catch the next one.' There would have been no hope about it. 'Make sure you catch the next. No excuses. Don't disobey me.' That's what she'd expected him to text.

She could still go, tell him she was catching a train to Liverpool airport and boarding the first available flight to Europe. Instead, she went to McDonald's in St Ann's Square. Ordered a black coffee and a double sausage and egg McMuffin. She had her own toiletries. Brushed her teeth. Gave herself a quick body wash. Cleaned fresh scars and scabs. Changed her underwear.

Back in the restaurant, she listened to shift workers talk about the gig economy. She envied their lives worrying about zero-hour contracts and bus timetables. Wished she had been born compliant with a normal family. She checked on train and flight times and almost booked, but there was still a nagging doubt. Leopards don't change their spots. She analysed the message Ed had sent her last night yet again. She wasn't sure he'd written it. The 'Nighty Night' was suspect. Normally he would spell it with an 'ie', getting off on the risqué innuendo about a sexy child's nightwear.

'Nightie nightie.'

She picked up the Daily Mirror and flicked through the pages. A disgraced former Prime Minster. War games in Ukraine. Rail strikes over pay and conditions. She could blame the missed train on the strikers if Ed asked why she wasn't halfway to Asia. Only problem, he was fastidious enough to check. She left the half chewed McMuffin on the plate and scooted across the city centre to the Malmaison.

In the hotel's foyer Alice flicked through the pages of the tabloid for a second time. She overheard snippets from passing staff and guests. Owen had allegedly beaten up his wife in a drunken, jealous rage. His anger had led to a heart attack. Alice glanced up from her newspaper. Peered into the breakfast room.

Someone was impersonating Ed really badly. Wore his wig like he'd placed a skunk on his head. His tailored clothes didn't hang on him like they should. Too many ruffles and creases and lumps. Vain Ed was always an immaculate dresser. She knew every inch of his body. Every sinew. Every mannerism. Every quirk. Every nuance. Every weird habit. It was the little things. Ed sawed slowly with his knife when he cut through meat. The imposter stabbed with his fork and ripped. Ed placed proportionate amounts on the fork. The imposter piled it high and fast and chewed with his mouth open. Ed never slumped or rested his elbows on the table, or rocked on his chair, or adjusted his wig because he wasn't used to it.

Slowly she got up from her seat and walked into the breakfast room. She told the waitress she would pay cash and sat several tables down from the girl and the imposter. Alice pretended to text friends and captured the duo on camera and video. She smiled at the imposter, who smiled back. Ed was embarrassed by his yellow, uneven teeth but was too old school to get them fixed. Real men didn't have cosmetic surgery. The imposter had a cheesecake grin with perfect teeth. Like the stranger with the beard who loitered outside the Swinging Vogue suite last night. Like Owen Chard on the internet.

They had killed Ed. Were they going to hijack her John Budd blackmail scam? Had Ed spilled the beans when he was pissed? Why else would Owen pretend to be Ed? There was no other reason.

Alice went to the toilet.

She locked herself in the cubicle, ripped off her jacket, flung off her top and sat on the toilet, knife in her hand. Tears rolled unchecked down her face and splashed on the floor between her feet. She was about to cut her flesh. A new three-inch wide gash on her left arm. Self-inflicted wounds stopped the pain in her head. Except she felt fine. She could cry on demand — always had the ability to turn on the waterworks. Poor old Ed. Died alone with two chancers for company. She smiled. Shook her head and put the knife away. Cried new tears of relief rather than grief. Free at last. He couldn't harm her or anyone else anymore.

NINETEEN

At nine thirty-five in the morning, Owen used Boucher's Uber app to book a ride to Central Park, Northampton Road, Newton Heath, Manchester. At nine forty the car drove him across the busy city to the police headquarters. Owen was met in reception by a middle-aged PR, Carol Cox. Her breath stank of garlic and booze and she said she would accompany him all the time he was at police headquarters, once he had signed in. Owen understood the reasoning. You couldn't have unsupervised civilians running around police stations uncovering racism, sexism and homophobia. He kept that comedic gem to himself. Carol explained that Ed would meet a detective this morning. After his briefing, they'd have lunch and then he could check John Budd's police and HR records. She would sit in with him. Copies couldn't be taken, for privacy reasons. The chief would have a chat afterwards. Explain why he had nominated his officer for the bravery award. 'Follow me,' she said.

They went up in a lift and walked at speed around a network of confusing corridors. If he had to escape in a hurry, he'd be buggered. The place was a maze of doors operated by a card access system. She moved too fast for small talk. She knocked on an interview room on the fifth floor and entered without waiting for an answer.

Detective Inspector Nigel Watts looked more like a chartered accountant than a senior Greater Manchester police officer. Clean shaven, thin and neatly dressed. Tie and top button done up. A suit that fitted. He wasn't covered in coffee spills and food stains, and didn't stink of beer, cigs and BO. Watts was tailor-made not to be in a crime novel franchise or a TV detective series. 'What are you going to give John Budd?' asked Watts, after the introductions were over, cutting right to the chase.

Owen played the transparency card. Transmitted the positivity the detective would want to hear. 'Strictly off-the-record, it's a George Cross. They're rarely given out because they are for acts of gallantry of the greatest heroism, the most conspicuous courage in circumstances of extreme danger,' said Owen. He sipped his coffee slowly and tried to keep his heartbeat normal. There was no leaving now, nowhere to run. But there was no reason for them to suspect anything, unless somebody had met the real Ed Boucher before.

'Is it the civilian equivalent of the Victoria Cross?' asked Watts.

'Yes, the same high criteria. The degree of the risk of death for the George Cross is over 90%. Other factors range from an awareness of danger, preparedness, persistence, third-party protection, saving life, injury and physical surroundings,' said Owen, regurgitating the notes he'd read earlier. He was good at learning lines sober.

'OK, here's why John Budd deserves the George Cross,' said Watts.

The chief asked me to brief you before he speaks to you because no one knows John Budd better than me. I've known him for over twenty years. I was his best man when he married Heather. I am godfather to his beautiful daughter, Hannah. I was with him over the weekend he was injured. As a key witness, I took no part in the investigation apart from giving a statement. I am also a trustee on his healthcare trust fund, along with Sir Richard, Buddy's neurosurgeon Helen Tapody, his wife Heather, daughter Hannah, and Jane Church, the editor of the local evening newspaper.

Last year a world title fight came to Manchester. Juke JJ Jones, our local boy, versus a bloody German monster, Wolfgang Muller. Me and John treat ourselves and book into the city's best hotel on a Thursday night for a very long, expensive, boozy, fun weekend. We both want JJ to win, obviously, but neither of us think he will. Out of loyalty, we place twenty quid bets on him to win and pick a KO round as a private wager for the beers after the bout. I took the first half of the fight; John took the second.

When we arrive at the hotel on Thursday, we meet up with this lovely couple, Salim and Zara. They are big fight fans, like me and Buddy. They invite us to their penthouse suite. We get on like a house on fire. We find we had a lot in common, despite very different cultural backgrounds. They claim to hire private planes to trot around the globe. Me and Buddy travel EasyJet on all-inclusive golfing holidays.

We take what they say with a pinch of salt. I'm not being racist, but there is a tendency for foreigners to exaggerate their wealth and influence. To be honest, they do have loads of gold tat and watches and heavy-duty jewellery in their suite. Salim said he was big in sport back home and had access to both boxers at the weigh-in on the Friday before the fight. He said he can invite us to the weigh-in tomorrow as his special guests and me and Buddy are dead chuffed.

Although we've met JJ numerous times down Harry Quinn's Moston gym, we've never been up close with the Eastern Beast, Wolfgang Muller esquire. Harry's a colourful character who used to manage JJ. Pay Per View TV bought out his contract, but Quinn still trains him. We're on nodding terms with Harry, but it's not good PR to be on his Xmas card list. He dances on the edge of a knife with lots of pretty unsavoury characters.

Enough of Harry. This is about John. The next night, we meet up again in their suite. Zara said she has a problem. The black shoes she wants to wear to the fight are missing. She swears blind she packed them when they flew in from Monte Carlo. Salim said red shoes, blues shoes, what does it matter? Zara replies shoes are everything. If your feet don't feel comfortable, your whole appearance is out of synch.

Buddy suggests nipping to the Trafford Centre to buy new black stiletto shoes. I'm disappointed. Salim said he still wants to meet Muller's and JJ's promoters before the fight to discuss rematch options in the Middle East. Once the fight is over, everyone will be getting smashed. Any rematch conversations would be put on hold for at least a month.

Buddy said he'll take her to the Trafford Centre. It is a great compromise. I suggest me and Buddy spoof for the off-duty 'bodyguarding' duties, but he says no. He volunteered, his idea. He calls a taxi to take them to the Trafford Centre.

Twenty minutes later, just as we were about to leave for the weigh-in, Buddy calls. Says a gun is pointed at Zara's head. Masked gunmen have hijacked their black cab. They want the valuables in Zara's hotel room. Take them to the bridge outside the hotel's front, a black cab will be waiting. Throw the bag into the back. Any police, and Zara is dog food. Salim begs Buddy to help make sure his wife isn't hurt. Over the phone we hear fighting. Then the line goes dead.

That's the last time I ever speak to my best friend. We've stitched this video together to show what happened next.

Distant CCTV footage from a local metal recycling business reveals the black cab is lost in a remote part of Salford Quays wasteland. Budd is forced out at gunpoint. The black cab drives up a dead end and doubles back. Buddy jumps on the front. The driver cannot see through the windscreen and hits a bollard at pace. Buddy limps towards the immobilised vehicle. One of the kidnappers, identified post mortem as Paul Quinn, fires shots. God is on Buddy's side. All six bullets miss. Buddy decks Quinn. Gets Zara out of the car just in time. You can also see a dazed Quinn try to help the driver. DNA identified him as Paul's cousin, 'Smoking' Stevie Quinn, nicknamed because he always had a tab in his mouth.

Buddy sees another black cab driving and hides Zara in the undergrowth. The crashed black cab is leaking petrol and catches fire. The Quinns have no chance once the fire takes hold.

After Budd hides Zara he calls 999. We've got the call on tape. Here's a snippet.

Operator: Police. How can we help.

Budd: This is John Budd. I am an off-duty police officer. Kidnapping taking place in Salford Quays near the junction of Waterways Avenue and Pomona Strand.

Operator: Are you involved?

Budd: Tried to kidnap my friend, Zara. Shots fired.

Operator: Are you safe?

Budd: Not really.

Operator: Can you hide?

Budd: I'm looking for a safe place.

Operator: The police are on their way. Is anyone else armed?

Budd: I don't know.

Operator: What was that noise?

Budd: A car exploded.

Operator: Are you OK?

Budd: I've hidden Zara in some trees. Shit. They've stopped. I'm running down to the waterfront to decoy the black cab. Hurry.

Operator: Take care.

Budd: I will.

Next time the CCTV picks him up he's hit by a second black cab that knocks him right off his feet. He gets up and the black cab u-turns and hits him again. We never knew the name of the man driving the second cab. It had fake number plates. We don't even have a suspect. All the kidnappers' mates were at a christening in Salford, with plenty of CCTV footage and mobile phones and Fitbits to prove they were there.

There are no words that capture my admiration for the bravery of my friend, and I trust you and the Queen and the Prime Minister feel the same way. A George Cross is the right way for a nation to say thank you.

TWENTY

Watts had dictated his thoughts to his mobile notes app in case he ever needed to jog his memory. Had he sold John Budd's bravery hard enough? Watts wasn't sure. How did a pen-pusher who had never been contaminated by a city's criminal underworld ever understand the life? How could you explain that the stench of the gutter never left your nostrils once you'd seen the damage people did to each other for crazy reasons like honour and respect. The cops who chased society's dregs weren't much better. Seemed like every week one of Watts' police colleagues was getting jailed for rape or sacked for gross misconduct for giving dirty colleagues a free pass. More annoying, the majority of his fellow cops were incompetent. Couldn't detect a crime if it happened under their noses. If you were good, you were seen as a threat by setting the standards too high. Crazy thing, everyone was equal when a lone trumpeter played the intro to the Crematorium Blues. What good was a bagful of money or a clean conscience when God wanted you, like that poor bastard who played Billy Whyte in *Northern Filth*? He snuffed it in the Malmaison without any warning. Mind, he shouldn't be too sympathetic. Wanker actors like him damaged the police as much as cops who raped and murdered private civilians. Not that anyone was interested in the cynical worldview of Nigel Watts. He was yesterday's news, seeing out his time. The scary prospect of retirement and a pension and becoming a full-time golfing grandfather loomed on the horizon. At least Watts had a future, no matter how dull. John Budd wasn't that lucky. JB wasn't going to see any retirement plans come to fruition. The silly bugger had destroyed not only his life, but the futures of his wife, Heather, and their young teenage daughter, Hannah. Budd was a prisoner in his own home with live-in carers dressing and cleaning him before they lifted him with a hoist into a semi-sitting position and shoved a telly in front of him.

Watts would visit them after this George Cross business was done and dusted. The good news would cheer Heather up. A trip to Buckingham Palace to meet the Queen. How good was that? Watts called around once or twice a week and would sit with his old friend and talk about the good old days, the lives they once enjoyed. Two desperadoes waiting for a train. Hannah had taken to sitting with her father too, said she was teaching John to communicate by blinking his eyes. Watts wasn't buying that, unsure if it was healthy for a teenager to isolate herself from her friends and peers. Watts knew Heather was equally isolated. John would brag to him about their healthy sex life, banging away like rabbits. Said their daily morning and nighttime shags protected his prostate. How was she coping with a 12-month enforced abstinence? JB couldn't service her anymore, nor could anyone else unless they were completely stupid. Not with the entire GMP force and social media watching. There was CCTV inside and outside the house that clocked every move. In a perfect world, they'd face up to John's reality. Problem was that humans weren't horses or old dogs. A mercy killing, no matter how humane and well intentioned, was still murder; the ultimate sin against God and his oath as a police officer.

Twenty-one

Owen washed his hands and face in the top floor executive toilet. He'd wasted an hour looking through John Budd's police records and pretending to take notes. Carol Cox had sat opposite him, spending the entire time texting. After the dress rehearsal with Nigel Watts, this was the big test. Could he fool the second most senior police chief in England with his live one-man Ed Boucher show? Sir Richard was the law-enforcement equivalent of film directors with multiple Oscars to their names.

Carol Cox took him into the chief constable's oak-panelled executive suite and did the introductions. The chief's breath stank as much as the hungover PR girl's, they shared the same unpleasant whiff of stale booze and garlic and the chief's eyes were equally bloodshot. Owen earwigged four senior male police officers who had carelessly spoken about their fallen heroic colleague. He might have heard the phrase 'half-man, half-vegetable', but he couldn't swear to it. 'Shall we take our seats, gentlemen?' said Sir Richard, gesturing for his guests to park themselves around a mahogany conference table. 'I think we should crack on.'

This was Owen's point of no return. He felt calm. His entire acting career was focused on this criminal moment. He made himself comfortable and imagined facing Marty Scorsese, Clint Eastwood and Francis Ford Coppola, his three favourite film directors. Sir Richard smiled at him. He coughed to clear his throat, ready to chair the meeting. Owen interrupted. 'No disrespect. This is a private and confidential conversation with the chief constable. We're not keeping minutes. Nor is anyone else invited or welcome to take part. No offence.'

The chief interrupted. 'Your office said I could invite whoever …'

'My office made a mistake.'

'You sent me an email.'

'This meeting is just for you and me, Sir Richard. I am here to assess your nomination letter and to run background checks on a nominee whose name cannot be made public or discussed beyond these four walls. My work is private and confidential. We have to protect the integrity of the Cabinet Office, the Prime Minster and, most importantly, HRH, and respect the rights of DC Budd and his family.' How good did that bullshit sound? If only the boys in the Dog and Duck could have seen him.

'We'll leave, Sir,' said one of the officers.

'Our lips are sealed,' said another.

'Ditto,' said the third.

'Are you sure that we can't sit in? John Budd is a colleague and a friend,' said the fourth.

'Everything is confidential and what is said in this room, stays in this room,' said Owen. 'Remember, absolutely no leaks, gentlemen. Her Majesty will be very upset if this turns into a soap opera.'

'What about me?' asked Carol.

'You too,' said Owen.

When they had gone, Owen told Sir Richard not to worry. It was an emotional time. He had seen the compelling evidence presented by DI Nigel Watts and there was no doubt John Budd was an extraordinary man. But that wasn't in question. 'Bravery medals are a rarity, not a right. "Exceptional bravery" are the key words when I write my report for the honours committee, "exceptional bravery" not undermined by "embarrassing behaviour" that might compromise the Crown. Do you understand?'

'I think I do,' said Sir Richard.

'Nobody expects our heroes to be saints, but we don't want them to be devils in disguise. That's why I needed to see John Budd's personal files and his disciplinary records. Make sure he pays his taxes and he's not a wanted man. Carol was very helpful. You must thank her.'

'Yes,' said Sir Richard, 'she is a wonderful person.'

'Now, tell me why you've put forward John Budd for a bravery award, specifically a George Cross. You can refer to your letter to refresh your memory.'

'I've done a PowerPoint I was going to show you and the team. Shall I …'

'Your words are fine, Sir Richard. If I had a pound for every PowerPoint I've sat through, I'd be on a beach in Barbados sipping gin and tonics with Mrs Ed, watching the cricket. I'm listening.'

Police officers have a tough job. Demands on their time, physically and mentally, are enormous, irrespective of whether they are frontline officers or managers working behind the scenes. There is no respite. You might be off-duty, not on the clock, but you're still a policeman or woman. You're still working even if you're not getting paid. You always have a responsibility to protect the public.

On occasions, we, as the police, are asked the ultimate question: would you put your life on the line? JB was asked that question and he stood up and was counted. An example to every young recruit who signs on the dotted line and takes the oath.

We know how bravely he answered that question. My colleague DI Watts has shown you how the events unfolded. My letter to the Cabinet Office and Sir Giles Thompson covers the same territory.

There are a lot of bad headlines about the police and how inept and useless we are. People love to laugh at us. Well, let them laugh, they can mock all they want. My response, 'what about John Budd?'

But how do we say thank you to John for his sacrifice? He no longer needs money, apart from his care, and we have plenty of cash in the bank thanks to a very generous general public. I can't promote him. He is not fit for police work and never will be.

That's why I would love to see the Queen pin a George Cross on John's chest. Nothing would make me more proud of my time in office than to be present when the nation celebrates a 24-carat gold hero.

TWENTY-TWO

Funny how lying was easier when you played somebody else. There was no guilt attached. because Ed Boucher was about to ruin Sir Richard's day and John Budd's heroic reputation, not Owen Chard. 'Very informative and heartfelt, Sir Richard. Now what I've got to say is strictly between us. You must swear you will never discuss it with anyone else,' said Owen.

'Swearing is a bit extreme. I am very religious man. Why?'

'If anyone knows I've had this conversation with you, I would be sacked and lose my civil service pension. You've really impressed me today and I am telling you this because I admire John Budd, and I too want him to get the George Cross.'

'What are you trying to say, Mr Boucher?'

'I have a predicament: a serious accusation has been made against Budd,' said Owen, lowering his voice for dramatic effect. 'I have a letter. I think you should read it,' said Owen. He handed Sir Richard Nurse A's statement.

The chief constable took it and read it quickly. 'Can I keep this as evidence?'

'No.'

'Do you mind if I read it out loud?' Owen couldn't think of a good reason to say no, so nodded yes.

To Whom It May Concern

Ive read in the Manchester Daily News that youre thinking of giving John Budd a bravery medal for saving that Arab woman. I am writing to tell you that far from being a hero he is a sexual predator and a rapist who left me anxious and suicidal.

I was a trained nurse but cannot work in hospitals anymore because of what has happened to me. I reported a domestic violence assault to the police who arrested and questioned my ex-husband. I was visited by two officers to discuss my complaint and whether I wanted to press charges against Nelson (that's not his real name in case you try and identify me without asking my permission). I didn't know what do to apart from I knew I could never have him back.

A week later the man I now know is John Budd knocked on my door totally uninvited. He said he was not an investigating officer on my case but he wanted to make sure I was safe from a further attack. At the time he said his name was 'Nigel'. He showed me his ID card and said I could call the station to verify him. Stupidly I took him at his word and let him in. I never looked at the ID card because I wasn't wearing my reading glasses. He walked around the house and made recommendations about making my home more secure. Locks on the windows. Double locks on my doors. CCTV inside and out. He gave me his mobile number. Said anytime I was scared, or Nelson turned up, just call. Said domestic bullies never took on real men.

Over the next month we would talk every day on the phone and he would visit to check I was alright. I realise now that what was happening was grooming. Initially, we sat on different chairs. Then he would sit on the same sofer as me. Hold my hand while we talked. Stroked my hair. Put his arm around me. I liked it. Made me feel comfortable. And very safe. He would kiss me on the cheek to reassure me. Then he moved to kissing my lips. Each time getting more intimate with his tongue to explore every corner and crevice of my mouth. Shocked as I was I didn't want his kindness to end.

All the time he is telling me how remarkable and strong I am and how pretty and attractive I am and I like him talking that way about me after Nelson robbed me of my worth. I tell him about the help I am waiting to receive from domestic violence counsellors and how I've been prescribed antidepressants from my doctor to cope with my anxiety and stress. He said he is falling in love and we should express our love physically. He said love making was a better cure than tablets prescribed by pharmaceutical companies looking to exploit vulnerable people like me.

We start to do that. Get physical. Intimate touching in the most private places, although we are still downstairs on the sofer. First through clothing. Then underneath clothing. Then bear. We laugh at his tattoos on his bum. Three lions on his left cheek the red devils on the right and the joker in the middle. Said he had them when he was a nipper.

This 'flirting' goes on for two weeks. He would arrive. Make a coffee. Ask how I was doing. And then we would start touching each other. He takes me to the edge numerous times and leaves me having to do myself fast as I can in a cold empty house when he had gone. He has this big uncircumcised penis with a weird boomerang kink when he had a hard on. He's much biggar than Nelson, even though my ex is from Jamaica.

Eventually, when our emotions hit fever pitch, we race upstairs. It was so unexpected we didn't have any protection. We have full sexual intercourse vaginally and anally. I'd never done anal before in my life. It hurts like crazy but I never felt so happy or more in love.

Finally I slept like a princess that night. Didn't wash his juices or his smell off me for a week. Every intimate part of my body throbbed a delicious mixture of pleasure and pain. I was desparate to see him so we could do it all over again, only longer and harder.

But once he got what he wanted he suddenly vanished from my life as quickly as he had entered it. I never saw or heard from him again. The mobile was never answered. I called the police and they said they had lots of officers called 'Nigel'. I went into a big depression and tried to kill myself and I lost my job and my home before I found Jesus. I even had an AIDS test because he had not used protection.

Next time I saw him was on TV and on the front page of the Manchester Daily News when he was hurt and recognised him immediately as 'Nigel'. That appeal made me sick to my core. Over a million pounds for a predator and rapist. And what do I get? Suffering and pain. All the memories came flooding back and I harmed myself again.

Please don't honour him when he is a bad bad man.

It is only because God intervened and saved me that I am writing this to you. As God is my witness this is my truth my whole truth nothing but my truth.

Yours 'Mandy'

PS: 'Mandy' is not my real name.

'Is it true? Have you verified it? Has she reported this to the police? Is there a police record with John named?' asked Hurst.

'Those questions are not our immediate issue, Sir Richard. At the moment, only two people know about this letter, apart from the poor soul who wrote it. Me and you, unless you advise otherwise today,' replied Owen.

'What are you suggesting?'

'Once an allegation is officially on the record, John Budd won't get his gallantry medal. The Queen cannot give awards to suspected rapists, no matter how brave they are or how weak the allegation is against them,' said Owen.

'That's outrageous. Absolutely stinks,' said Hurst.

'I sympathise, but I am only doing my job. I'm putting my good name on the chopping block for John Budd. If this slips out, you would survive. Me, I'd be ostracised for embarrassing the Queen. She would blame me personally if I betrayed her trust. That's why I asked everyone else to leave. You understand now why I went against previous protocols?'

'What do we do?' asked Hurst.

'Your call. I'll follow your lead.'

'What lead?'

'We have two choices. We can do the so-called "right thing",' said Owen.

'What does that mean?'

'I speak to my line manager about the letter. Once it is official, the Independent Office for Police Conduct will investigate. This nomination process is postponed indefinitely until we dismiss the allegations beyond any reasonable doubt and show John Budd is completely innocent of any sexual abuse offences and misconduct in a public office,' said Owen, ad-libbing like he had a small but vital part in a Mike Leigh kitchen sink drama.

'Is this for real?'

'Sadly, yes.'

'What's the second choice?'

'We compensate her,' said Owen, making sure he said his words carefully and slowly.

'Never. Never succumb to blackmailers,' said Hurst.

'I don't think it is blackmail really. It's compensation for John Budd's sexual abuse.'

'It's bloody blackmail.'

'Let's not get lost in definitions. You, not me, can decide to pay her off to protect John's family from any further stress and anxiety,' said Owen. He used Budd's first name to imply a deeper personal connection with the brain-damaged officer.

'Over my dead body,' said Sir Richard, his face puce. He banged the table. Coffee splashed over mahogany. Biscuits skated across the polished wood. 'How do we get in touch with her?'

'I've already spoken to her,' said Owen.

'You have? I'd like to speak to her too. You got her number? We can easily disprove it when she gives us dates and a location and her mobile number,' said Hurst.

'I promised her anonymity,' said Owen. 'Promised her everyone would sign a non-disclosure agreement to protect her for infinity.'

'You don't have that authority.'

'I do,' said Owen. He was coming to the money shot and was revelling in his show-stopping performance.

'This is totally insane. How can you suggest...?'

'Paying her off?'

'Yes. That's against the law, against everything I believe in. How dare you come into my office and suggest such an outrage?'

'I'll contact my manager. Obviously, I won't mention our chat. You're doing the right thing, Sir Richard,' said Owen. He slowly closed his notebook. Placed it and the folder back in his briefcase. He pulled at his shirt sleeves, stood up and offered his hand for the chief constable to shake.

'I'd like to say it's been a pleasure meeting you, but we both know that would be a lie.' Reluctantly they shook hands. This cat-and-mouse game was better than any pretend movie set. There was one major problem. The chief wasn't buying his proposition.

'It's not personal. Just a job,' said Owen.

'Damn men and their bloody boomerang peckers,' muttered Sir Richard, under his breath, loud enough for Owen to hear. Owen stood up.

'Nobody's perfect.' Owen took a slightly damp bourbon biscuit from the tabletop and bit into it, buying himself precious time for Sir Richard to see the light. He pushed his chair back under the table, smiled at the chief constable and headed towards the door. Five more steps. His hand grabbed the cold brass door handle and he opened it. He felt a rush of fresh cool air. The chief's office was very stuffy, Owen had been too focused on the hustle to notice. 'Goodbye.'

'Wait,' said Sir Richard.

Twenty-three

Damn, damn and bloody double damn. Sir Richard's career in the police was at risk, thanks to an officer who couldn't keep his trousers zipped. What was wrong with people? He'd only got this job because nobody had checked his CV too closely and the previous chief led a force that failed to log eighty thousand crimes. How did you manage to be that shit?

Any story breaking about a John Budd cover-up, no matter how small, would inevitably lead to his resignation or early retirement. On the surface, what John Budd had done was hardly the crime of the century. But JB would have been dismissed for forming an inappropriate sexual relationship with a vulnerable woman he'd met while pretending to be on duty. Budd more than likely had also illegally accessed police computer systems, obtained personal information about Nurse A's reports of domestic violence, and then impersonated another officer.

If any part was true, it was catastrophic. Sir Richard knew he should call the Independent Office for Police Conduct while Ed Boucher was in the room. But it was so unfair. How many more humiliations for Hurst? How many more apologies for a police force that failed women, teenagers and children? How many more millions did the force have to pay out for their incompetence? At least with this banana skin, he had options. Question was, could he trust Ed Boucher? 'Come back in and sit down,' said Hurst.

'OK.' Owen did as he was told.

Sir Richard walked to a window and looked out over the city. Manchester enriched him on one hand, impoverished him on the other. If they accused him of perverting the course of justice, would they take back his knighthood? Hurst should ask Boucher. He would know. Except the sooner the vain creep with the wig and ultra-white teeth left his office, the better. 'How can we trust each other if I agree to what you're suggesting?' Hurst asked.

'I'm retiring soon. I've done this once and we kept it a secret. These are exceptional circumstances,' said Owen.

'And the nurse? What would she do?'

'Everyone signs an NDA. Protects us all. And she trusts me and hates you and what you represent.'

'Why you?'

'Friendly face and winning personality?'

Sir Richard wanted to smash the civil servant in the face, because he was taking the piss out of him and the police badge. 'How much?'

'A quarter of a million quid in non-traceable diamonds,' said Owen.

Sir Richard laughed and banged the table. The coffee cup was virtually empty but coffee spilled from the saucer onto the wood. 'Sorry to get Anglo-Saxon. She can fuck off and stuff her diamonds up her arse. You can too,' said Hurst.

'Don't shoot me,' said Owen. 'I'm just a piggy in the middle, no derogatory pun intended. I've spoken to her. I asked what would it take for her to retract her letter. She gave me her price. She could be talking codswallop for all I know. But when I write my report, I'll have to know whether to include the allegation or not. Your call, chief constable.'

Hurst shook his head and said, hypothetically speaking, if he was to consider compensation, he would never get it approved by Greater Manchester's police and crime commissioner and her team. And if he did, it would take months, if not years. 'I won't be able to find a quarter of a million pounds in uncut diamonds,' said Hurst.

Owen smiled at the chief. 'I believe John Budd's healthcare trust fund has a million quid in it. I also believe you are chair of the trustees. Nobody will ever know, if you brief your accountants. Delay the accounts for as long as you can!'

'I don't often dislike people when I first meet them. Normally it takes time for me to find them abhorrent. With you it's instant, Mr Boucher. You're not fit to shoeshine John Budd's boots,' said Hurst.

'You're talking to the wrong man, chief. Like I said, I'm a messenger, not your white whipping boy,' replied Owen. 'Let's exchange mobile numbers. Call me when you have the compensation and are ready to sign the NDA. Anyone else gets involved and our deal is off. I am not going to be crucified because you couldn't organise a piss up in a brewery, even if you do smell like one.'

The chief watched Boucher leave and had already made up his mind. He would see if Watts could find the nurse and debunk the abuse and rape allegations. If not, he would make sure he was protected, mentally and financially. Was it time for a career change? It was OK being top dog, but it was lonely and stressful. Banging junior staff was the only perk when everybody else wanted to have your head rather than give it. What he wanted in the prime of his life was sand, sea and sex, and no taxes.

Twenty-four

Marks out of ten? An eight, maybe a seven. Owen had definitely lost it when the chief's hypocritical pomposity hacked him off. He was unable to stop himself breaking character and becoming a combination of Vic Savage and Billy Whyte for a second or two.

In the lift, neither Owen nor Carol spoke. She'd picked up on the chief's bad vibes. She waited in the foyer until a black cab arrived and left without a goodbye.

What were the odds on getting the compensation? Was he warm or cold? You could never tell how you did in an audition. They always said nice things until you were out of the rehearsal room. Then you waited. Hours, days, sometimes weeks, while they hedged their bets on the availability of their preferred choices.

In the black cab, Honest Norman was a fan when Owen said he had been reading about John Budd. 'John Budd is a bloody legend. What a fighter, what a man, what a hero. Us drivers had a whip round that weekend and raised a couple of grand, hat was filled instantly.'

'That's good of you.'

'A gut reaction mate. A few cynical cabbies say it was an inside job. Me, I'm not sure. Not living off the proceeds of ill-gotten gains, is he? Saw him a few months back on the TV. Looks bloody dreadful, worse than my old man and he's got that dementia brain disease where he can't recognise his own son or control his bladder. If my old man was a dog, he'd be at the vets for a lethal injection, no questions asked. Same with John Budd.'

'Could you do it? Euthanise your own flesh and blood?'

Honest Norman looked in the rearview mirror and gave Owen his best John Wayne impersonation. 'Sometimes a man's gotta do what a man's gotta do.'

'That's not what John actually said in Stagecoach,' said Owen.

'Who cares? It's close enough,' said Norman. 'Why split hairs? You know what I meant.'

'I do, indeed,' Owen gave Big Norman that rebuke for free. He needed a pint or two. Blackmail was stressful. Waiting for the outcome was unbearable sober and there was an abortion to come. Maybe he needed three pints.

Twenty-five

Nigel Watts loitered around the sixth floor and made small talk with the executive admin staff. Chatted about boxing, football, the high cost of living, the war in Ukraine and Big John. The conversation always, inevitably, navigated towards John Budd. How was he doing? Stable, very stable. Was he improving? No, not really. Can he communicate? Sadly, no. How were wife Heather and daughter Hannah coping? As best as anyone could expect in the circumstances. Would he walk again? Watts was no medical expert, but John was being looked after by the best healthcare professionals in Manchester.

There was always one question left unasked. They shot injured horses, put them out of their misery.

A breathless Carol Cox arrived on the executive floor, knocked and went straight in. She emerged ten seconds later from the chief constable's executive suite with Ed Boucher. The civil servant followed her out. Hurst did not accompany them to the lift like he normally did with guests.

What was going on?

Watts acknowledged Boucher, the civil servant smiled with capped teeth and a dead rat perched precariously on his head. Maybe he was a divorcee or a widower, too inept to buy clothes that fitted. His classic 'old school' clobber looked expensive enough, except everything was a little too short.

Sir Richard Hurst was usually calm under pressure, that was one of the reasons he was the region's top cop. Sir Richard had an instinctive ability not to let anger cloud his judgement. Most people thought it was a talent but Watts knew better. Hurst was as thick as a brick but was good at managing meetings and reading out loud in public. 'Did John Budd fuck around?' asked Hurst.

Watts wondered what shagging had to do with acts of bravery. If extra-marital affairs disqualified you from senior roles, then Sir Richard was in trouble. Carol Cox was his current squeeze, the last of a long line of gullible females seduced by the power of office. 'Are you serious? John loved his wife as often as possible,' said Watts.

'What you're about to hear is strictly confidential. Not a word to a soul. Not even Frankie. I don't want her psychoanalysing us, trying to make sense of this madness. I need your head to be uncluttered. Am I clear?'

'Sure,' nodded Watts.

'Say it,' demanded Hurst.

'Yes. Very clear.'

The chief played Nigel a recording of him reading Nurse A's letter, outlining her allegations against John Budd. He said he'd WhatsApp a copy to him, but it must stay confidential. 'Does that sound like your friend?' asked Hurst.

'No. What's going on?' asked Watts. Big John was in big trouble.

'I don't know. I want you to find out for me. Off the clock. Off the record. Just you. A lone wolf gig. Report back direct to me. Check out Ed Boucher. Find Nurse A. Find out if there are legs in the allegation. You've got twenty-four hours, maybe forty-eight at a push.'

'Before?'

'John loses his George Cross,' said Hurst.

'Or we pay compensation?' asked Watts. 'How much?'

'A quarter of a million quid.'

Watts laughed out loud. Wondered how Boucher and his nurse had arrived at that figure. Not the easiest amount of money to launder through the police budgets. 'From…?'

'His trust fund. Me and you can disguise the transaction from the others for as long as we want, delay audits for months and years. Call it medical consultation and security payments over time,' said Hurst.

'Let's disturb the bottom of the pond first. Do I have to play nice?'

'Play as dirty as you want but keep it honest. This ever leaks out, we're toast. So minimal notes and records unless we have a chance of convicting Boucher. Understand?'

'When are you going to call him next?'

'Depends if you find Nurse A,' said Hurst. 'You know he called me a hypocrite? Can you believe that?'

Watts couldn't. Well, he could. Everyone was a hypocrite. It was impossible not to be one. Humans weren't designed to be morally perfect. 'That's pen pusher southerners for you,' said Watts.

'Don't let me down Nigel. This is strictly between you and me for the time being. Nobody else needs to know. You're the most honest cop on the force. More honest than the force's padre. You're so inscrutable, you should be Japanese.' The chief winked at Watts, who grinned back at the racist idiot. Behind his PR facade, Hurst was a self-obsessed disingenuous fraud. Too many people in power were like him. Was Watts tainted by association? He hoped not. A good cop was the master of his own reputation. He could never justify crossing the invisible line in the sand that would make him as corrupt and crooked as the criminals he chased. This investigation would follow the same modus operandi as any other he led. Others higher up the food chain would have to decide to pull it. He wasn't going to carry the can.

TWENTY-SIX

Free rein with the chief constable's blessing, if Watts kept it honest with minimal notes. Watts dictated his thoughts into his mobile notes app. He was the chief's 'just in case' insurance policy. The chief had already decided Watts' findings would never be shared with the CPS. Hurst would pay up to protect his and Budd's reputations, whatever the cost.

Watts would Code 66 his detective mates, soon as he knew what needed to be investigated. Code 66 was an open invitation for his mates to unofficially help each other.

He called his wife, Frankie, and told her he was working late. Headed north out of Manchester's city centre, up the Bury New Road towards Prestwich. Three miles later, he turned right into St Mary's Road, left into Church Lane and then right again to the top of Crusader Avenue and the middle terrace on the left. John lived there with wife Heather, daughter Hannah, and a permanent live-in carer who had a two-hour afternoon break when another carer sat in with John in case of an emergency. There was double-up duty four times a day for feeding and personal care.

Nigel had his own key to the green front door. He let himself in to the double-fronted middle-terrace and shouted hello. Didn't want to frighten the occupants. He walked through the lounge door. The TV was on but nobody was watching. Through the swing doors in the living room, he could see a shadow in John's bedroom. He knocked on the door and entered to find Hannah, still in her purple school uniform, sitting with her dad and reading to him. Hannah pointed to the ceiling, silently informing Watts her mum was upstairs in the attic living room. The two females called it their sky-high sanctuary to escape the omnipresent care circus below

Watts went up, knocked and entered. Heather was sipping coffee as she watched the telly, laid out on a sofa in a jumper and jeans. Fingers tucked into the top of her tight denims. She muted the box. John and Heather had been triathletes, effortlessly running, cycling and swimming long distances. Right now, she looked like she'd struggle to run a bath. She looked pleased to see him but in the 12 months since the incident she had aged a decade and always looked exhausted without the war paint. She was probably eating too little, drinking too much and not training. She'd signed off sick as a staff nurse at North Manchester general hospital. She had worked there with Frankie half a dozen years ago, running eye clinics, helping the near-blind to see a bit better. Then Frankie had seen the light and wanted to explore the mind. Every time he came around to see Heather he started with the same conversation opener. 'How are you doing today?'

'I think I'm OK. My mask is good,' said Heather. 'Only slipped once or twice. My dilemma is what to wear for the boxing on Saturday. A black or white dress or maybe red? They're too tight now I'm putting on a few extra pounds!' Heather and Hannah were guests of honour, representing John Budd in front of thousands of boxing fans in the AO Arena. Millions more would watch on Pay Per View. The duo would be introduced before the main bout of the night.

'Have you got ringside seats?'

'A PR woman called Samantha Sparrow rang. Said we're in the VIP area. Said half a million has already been transferred into the trustee account. Salim and Zara will do the photo opportunity with us in the ring. Sir Richard is our chaperone.'

'That's very generous of them all,' said Watts.

'Samantha and a film crew are coming tomorrow to record our story. I couldn't say no after they were so generous,' said Heather.

'Any publicity helps fundraising,' said Watts. He looked across at the three dresses hung on a dado rail. Heather's eyes followed his.

'Which dress would you pick?'

'Blood splatter would ruin a white cocktail dress.'

'Blood stains would be a dramatic story for the grandkids one day,' said Heather. 'They aren't too sexy? Too provocative? Inappropriate?'

'A tough decision,' Watts said.

'Are you going?'

'Yes. I've had two tickets since the rematch was announced. Hoped the big man could come to the fight.'

'They wanted him to appear in the ring as well, but we don't want to drown in an ocean of self-pity,' said Heather.

Watts nodded. The Arabs and east Europeans would use the cheque presentation to make themselves look good. Classic sports washing that rinsed over human rights abuses and illegal invasions of sovereign states. He rarely shared his political opinions. The police should be impartial, like the Army, Navy and Air Force. He was a bloody pragmatic idealist, that was his problem. 'Apart from deciding what to wear for the boxing, any other problems?'

'The usual crap. Hannah's obsessed with reading to him. Thinks he can communicate through blinking. The live-in carer has an online boyfriend making her frisky. Helen Tapody's team are here every day. They turn the cameras off when they're in the room. Part of his rights to privacy. I'm kept in the dark. Whenever they do personal care, off goes the CCTV and I just get the audio. All these people drive you nuts. They keep telling me I've just got to be a little patient. I know I'm going to sound like a bitch. But who's looking after my needs?' asked Heather. 'I've gone from shagging twice a day to being celibate. Worn out three Rabbits, but it's not the same as having that huge cock inside me.'

'He used to call it his Big Banana because it kinked hard left and hard right. Loved anal because it was so tight,' lied Watts. Would Heather contradict him and confirm JB was a back-passage prude?

'Not like you to talk dirty, Nigel. Frankie opening her legs enough for you?'

There was an awkward silence. Heather could be crude, and he felt unusually embarrassed. Time to change the subject.

'Strictly between you and me, we had a visitor from the Cabinet Office to rubber-stamp John's George Cross,' said Watts.

'What's John going to do with one of them? Lick it? Stick it on the fridge?' asked Heather.

'Have you got John's phone and computer and any passwords?'

'Why do you want those?'

'Routine background checks,' said Watts.

'Go and see John. I'll fetch the devices after a cold shower. Salacious talk gets a girl all frothy.'

Downstairs, Watts interrupted Hannah. The teenager left him alone with her father and made a cup of tea with the live-in carer. Watts heard them chat about online boyfriends. Hannah said don't be fooled, they were probably fat seventy-year-old Russian eunuchs. Hannah was an astute young girl with a black sense of humour. Probably came with the territory when tragedy robbed you of the best years of your life.

Although Budd's bedroom had cameras on 24-hours-a-day in case John had a fit or a seizure, they could be turned off in his room when personal care was taking place. Watts flicked the switch to turn off the CCTV. He spoke quietly to John. 'You've created a right old mess here John, and yours truly has to sort it out again. You've got scammers trying to steal from your trust fund. They're accusing you of rape. Is it true? I pray to God you weren't that stupid, John.'

As Watts was about to leave, Heather came downstairs with the mobile phone, laptop and lots of leads. She handed the box to him, hugged him goodnight and leaned towards his left ear. 'John must have been teasing you. His Big Banana wasn't for every hole. John hated anal, unlike me. What about Frankie? Are you two fans?'

Heather smiled at him and stroked his arm. A major inaccuracy in the allegation letter. If one bit was fake, it was all fake.

TWENTY-SEVEN

Alice watched the tall redhead say goodbye to the man impersonating 'Ed'. Followed her into the city centre and thought she looked a happy soul. Ed's death last night didn't appear to weigh heavily on her mind. In St Ann's Square, the redhead hooked up with a chubby smoking woman. Alice followed them into King's Street. They made their way up some stairs into an office suite above a surfer accessories shop. Alice gave them five minutes before going to the entrance. There was a brass plate that said, the Manchester Ukrainian Refugee Centre.

Alice went into a nearby Factory Coffee Shop and ordered coffee. She exchanged a tenner for coins and googled the MURC and dead war journalists while she waited.

Alice returned to the office suite. Buzzed the entrance intercom. A voice answered. Alice asked if this was the place to make cash donations on behalf of the Ukraine war effort. She walked up the stairs. Two women were sitting in reception, surrounded by unopened parcels and envelopes. 'My name is Alice. I'm on a creative writing course at Manchester University. Me and my students were discussing Ukraine journalists killed in the war last night. We were in bits about the murders of cameraman Evgeni Sakun, photographer Maks Levin and journalist Oleksandra Kuvshinova and so many others. We had a whip round. We don't mind how you spend it.'

'That's very kind,' said the receptionist who introduced herself as Elina. Alice reached into her rucksack and brought out an envelope packed full of used twenties, tens and fivers and several bags full of coins. 'How much is there?'

'I've not counted. Shall we do it now? I'll need a receipt,' said Alice.

'Sure, Nina will sign it for it for you,' said Elina. 'I'll call her. Would you like a coffee?'

'Tea, if you're making it.'

They counted the money three times until they were satisfied they had an accurate total of seven hundred and seventy four pounds and 63 pence. After the third reconciliation, Nina popped out of her office and handed Elina a piece of paper. She introduced herself as the chief operating officer of the refugee centre. Nina said her charity could only survive on the generosity of people like Alice and her student friends. Behind Nina, the redhead stood in the doorway looking straight at her with blue-green eyes shining. She smiled and Alice smiled back, stunned by how young and beautiful she was close up. 'Hi.'

'Hi.'

'Alice is a university student in Manchester. She and her friends have donated cash to help refugees,' said Elina.

'Creative writing and journalism,' said Alice. 'I'll be famous one day. Alice Lamb-Percy. Never forget the name. Yours?'

'Angelina Kozar. I was a journalist back home,' said the redhead, 'before the war.'

'Would you come and talk to us?'

Angelina smiled and half-blushed at the invitation. 'I am going home soon.'

'Before you ask, I am too busy,' laughed Nina. 'We are grateful for everything the English people are doing for us.'

'What about coffee, Angelina?' asked Alice.

'Call me,' said Angelina. She gave Alice her number. 'Your face looks familiar. Have we met before?'

'No,' said Alice, who realised Ed might have carried snaps of her and

Lucy and Irene in his wallet. She was a lot different now with her tattoos, piercings and short hair.

Nina signed the receipt and handed it to Alice, who thanked her and put the paper down. She asked if she could take a selfie, encourage others to donate. She took out her mobile. Nina said it was fine for her as the public face of the charity, but the others were volunteers.

'I don't mind,' said Angelina.

'Nor me,' said Elina.

Alice snapped a couple of selfies. Angelina and Alice, arms around each other, flanked by Nina and Elina. Girl power. Survivor power. Alice thanked them all again, picked up the receipt and the other piece of paper Nina had handed to Elina, then realised her deliberate mistake when she read, 'Contact the Manchester unplanned pregnancy advisory service in south Manchester for an emergency termination.' She apologised and handed the note back to Elina. Alice had been on pill since her early teens, the day after Ed first had her. Only fools got pregnant by mistake and Angelina looked sensible enough. Poor Angelina.

Twenty-eight

Alice parked the pregnant Ukrainian refugee and focused on Samantha Sparrow. Did Samantha know they were related? Had she spooked Ed by mentioning they were stepsisters? Was that why he was so keen for her to fuck off to Europe?

Alice route marched across the city centre and hung around the back entrance of the Dakota hotel. She watched the staff pop outside for quick fag breaks. They came out in two or threes. Eventually one came out by herself and Alice walked across. Asked if the young woman had a light. Dani said she did. They smoked and chatted about agency work in Manchester and the best places to work where the tips were tidy.

Alice watched the cig burn down. A barometer for the time she had to pitch her access request with Dani. The Italian was from a small village overlooking Lake Como. She wanted to open a fashion boutique, if she found the right man to back her. They laughed at their social immobility in a male dominated world. 'How would you like to earn a hundred quid for looking the other way for a couple of minutes? Put it towards your retail investment fund? I'll give fifty to anyone else helping me,' said Alice. It cost her three hundred to bribe the hotel staff to gain access to Samantha Sparrow's penthouse suite.

According to the cleaning staff, the executive suites either side of Sparrow's were booked to accommodate a four-strong security team. Dani said they were scary muscle who worked for the head of Baltic Power. He would be staying in the suite on Saturday night. The security guys would get all frisky if they caught a cleaning girl alone. Alice asked if Dani was scared working with predators. No, she replied, the secret was to never stand still. Boxing helped too. Dani adopted an on-guard stance, jabbed a right an inch short of Alice's chin. They laughed.

Alice watched Samantha and her entourage from her observation point next to the cleaning cupboard at the far end of the landing. Samantha was never by herself long enough for Alice to approach, so she revised her plans. Alice would search her room when Samantha and her entourage left for a boxing PR conference.

When the coast was clear, Dani cleaned while Alice snooped. There were two en suite bedrooms in the hotel penthouse. Dani said the smaller of the two was occupied by Samantha. The larger rooms were for Baltic's Viktor Andreyev. Alice sniffed Sparrow's pillows before Dani changed the bed linen, Samantha stank of the menopause. Her wardrobe contained expensive designer outfits and sexy underwear. Alice nicked a dress, cashmere cardigan and a matching bra and pants, and put them in her rucksack. In the en suite, the cabinet had HRT replacement and anti-anxiety tablets alongside toothpaste, an electric toothbrush and luxury bubble bath. Alice was about to leave when she randomly rifled through Samantha's dirty laundry and half inched a used pair of black knickers. She felt a compulsive urge to check Samantha's DNA to confirm the older woman really was her half-sister.

Alice heard the door, Dani was coming to tell her to hurry up. She walked into the suite's main reception area smiling but Dani wasn't there. The giant who had picked Samantha up from the train station was standing there in a black suit and open neck white shirt. Alice had most recently seen him at Piccadilly train station. Before that, when he left a Kensington town house moments after Rupert Sparrow dive-bombed out of a fourth-floor window. The giant hadn't seen Alice hidden between two cars as he calmly walked away with another man and woman three steps behind him. Hadn't noticed her video him and his accomplices. 'Who are you?' he asked.

'Alice Lamb-Percy,' she said, admiring his chiselled beauty. 'You?'

'Stretch. What's in your hand, Alice?' asked the giant.

'Knickers.'

'Yours?' asked Stretch.

'Samantha's. I'm on the rag.'

'Rag?'

'Period. Bleeding down there,' said Alice. She gripped her vulva. Left her hand there longer than necessary.

'You English girls are so charming,' said Stretch.

'We try hard. Does it make you hard? Rag talk?'

'This makes me hard. I am carrying an automatic handgun, one used by a lot of bodyguards. The Sig Sauer P229 is easily concealed, but still packs a powerful punch with high caliber .357 hollow point rounds.'

'Wow,' said Alice.

'Normally this weapon is defensive, not aggressive. In the hands of someone like me, it is perfectly safe and will not hit the wrong people. Normally, I will group an average firing pattern less than two inches diameter when fired by hand from ten paces.'

'I reckon we're twenty at the moment,' said Alice. 'This is a big suite.'

'The hollow bullets will expand inside you for about a depth of twelve to eighteen inches and do far more damage than regular bullets,' said Stretch.

'Bang, bang. I am brown bread.'

'Normally I will put five to ten shots inside you rather than a single bullet. We're not on the television or in the movies where one shot drops a man,' said Stretch.

'Good thing I'm only a woman. Wouldn't you rather fuck than shoot me?' asked Alice.

'I use a segmented titanium 9mm suppressor to avoid any unnecessary noise.'

'You've got a great chat up line, Fritz,' said Alice, realising his sense-of-humour by-pass was probably autism.

'Stretch. I told you my name. I have diplomatic immunity, but I don't flash my weapon around. People get very nervous. But you don't. You aren't worried, Alice.'

'I have an undiagnosed antisocial personality disorder. Are you familiar with the term?'

'No.'

'Means I'm nuts and behave very differently to everyone else. You can bash me. Beat me up. I like it,' said Alice.

'Are you laughing at me, Alice?' Stretch asked.

Alice walked towards him slowly. Toyed with the black knickers. Stood under his armpit. Stretch took the knickers. Sniffed them like a wine buff smelling a cork for flaws. His eyes were locked on hers. He grinned at her. She grinned back. Was he going to make a move on her or should she go first? Stretch was hard as Blackpool rock. She lightly brushed over his cock. Clicked the blade. Watched the startled fear on his face. 'Too much chat. Not enough sexual violence,' said Alice. 'I want you to hurt me.'

'You wouldn't,' said Stretch.

'Try me.'

Stretch's hand gripped Alice's wrist. She knew he could snap it in two whenever he wanted. She no longer had the leverage to stab him. Not that she was going to. She felt his hand tenderly push her sleeve up her arm. His fingers gently ran over her scars. Like he was reading braille. Her free hand snuck up his sleeve. Felt old scars. 'You're a cutter,' said Stretch.

'Eases my pain. You?'

'Sometimes,' said Stretch.

'What about fucking?' asked Alice, taking out her mobile to film herself being stretched by Stretch.

'Shall we find out?'

TWENTY-NINE

Five minutes later, Alice ran down the landing. She took off her uniform and left it by the cleaning cupboard, waved goodbye to the girls and raced off down the stairs. Stretch had been quick and painful but she had his number. Men were different after they had puffed the dust. Treated you differently, casually.

Alice was lucky. She picked up the fake Ed Boucher trail at police headquarters. She sat outside in a black cab and asked her driver to follow his taxi when it appeared at the gate. They followed Owen into the city centre. The black cab dropped him outside the Unicorn pub, one of Manchester's less salubrious waterholes.

Alice followed him inside the pub. Owen, disguised as Ed, was sitting in the corner, his glass nearly empty. Pub's regulars discussed the soap opera actor's untimely death. One of the drinkers had met Owen many moons ago, when they were filming *Northern Filth* at Granada TV. He was drinking in the Cyprus Tavern, a spit-and-sawdust nightclub in Princess Street that hosted blue-light cops-and-nurses nights on Tuesdays. 'He stood his round. A good egg. When he got pissed he had an edge.'

Owen finished his pint and walked around the corner down Oldham Road into Manchester's Piccadilly Gardens. He headed up Portland Street towards the Malmaison hotel, where he ordered another pint and found a table far from the maddening boxing crowd five-deep around the bar. A text arrived. 'In Paris. WYWH. Fly 2 Bangkok tomorrow.' He stared at Ed's mobile but didn't reply.

Alice went to the toilet and put on Sparrow's expensive underwear and dress. It changed her appearance and the light blue cashmere jumper hid the scars and scabs on her arms.

Moments later Alice asked Owen if the spare chair was free. He nodded and shifted his legs. She put her glass of wine and her book — Emma Haughton's *The Dark* — on the table. 'Are you here for the fight?' Alice asked.

'No, business,' Owen replied. 'You?'

'I've come to pay my respects to the actor who died in this hotel. I know he's old enough to be my dad, but I loved him.'

'My condolences. Did you know him personally?'

'Only through his work. Billy Whyte in *Northern Filth*. Vic Savage in the punk-band Savaged by Sheep. Me and a schoolfriend called the group Shagged by Sheep. We fantasised about threesomes, with him ramming us. Do you remember that song about drugs and falling asleep and almost dying and the shock of finding your lover comatose?'

'You're talking to the wrong man!' said Owen.

'What do you mean?'

'That's what Billy used to say. It was his catchphrase. You're talking to the wrong man.'

'Sorry. My medication. My name's Alice.'

'No worries. I'm Ed,' Owen said.

'Pleased to meet you, Ed.'

They chatted about Owen's early work as a musician and she sang the *Sorry, I Made You Cry When I Almost Died* chorus. They replenished their glasses and Alice told him she was doing a novel writing MA at the University of Manchester. She asked him what he did, and he said he was a civil servant. Nothing as exciting as being a novelist. What was she writing about? She said *Truth Hurts* was about a young, privileged girl who hurts the ones she loves to find herself. Her journey was to find her real identity. Although she had two families, she never felt loved as a child once her mother disappeared.

93

'Sounds very serious. Real or imagined?' Owen asked.

'It's a semi-serious fictional satire,' Alice said, 'at least I hope it is. My tutor's sitting on the fence.'

'Do you like Japanese? There's a great restaurant in Piccadilly Gardens,' said Owen.

'I was thinking about eating in your hotel room upstairs?'

Three hours later Owen was in a deep drug-induced sleep and Alice was blissed out on the bed. Ed's things were all around her. Ed's clothes. Ed's luggage. Ed's briefcase. Ed's phone. Alice could still smell Ed in the room, on his clothes and his aftershave and body spray despite her own body being saturated in Owen's juices. She picked up Ed's mobile and keyed in the six-digit password. She put the AirPods into her ears and watched Angelina Kozar quiz Ed about rape, heard Ed beg for help. Angelina ignored his pleas and let him die. Alice felt nothing. What was wrong with her? She couldn't tell right from wrong, distinguish truth from lies, facts from fiction. And she couldn't trust her own memory of what she had done and who she was. It was like she already had dementia. Like Irene, her delusional grandma with her loud accusations about Lucy's death that Ed had silently believed too but never articulated, like the coward he was.

Thirty

DI Nigel Watts strode into the foyer of the Malmaison hotel and flashed his police ID at reception. He asked to speak to Michael Myles, the general manager. The receptionist said he was busy, would he like to speak to the duty floor manager? Watts said if Michael was in the building, he wanted a word, now. Told her they were old friends as pleasantly as he could without snapping. A couple of minutes later, Watts was sitting in Michael's plush office, surrounded by framed photographs of famous music, TV and sports legends with the hotel's genial general manager. 'How are things?'

'Apart from a soap star dropping dead, everything is dandy,' replied Myles. 'We expected press, but no one turned up. Is this social or work?'

'Both. I'd like to see the hotel records and any CCTV footage you have of Owen Chard and Ed Boucher in the hotel,' said Watts.

'Got a warrant?' joked Myles. He tapped into the hotel booking and F&B systems. 'Paperwork, in case head office asks stupid questions.'

'It's unofficial. I've never asked for any of this.'

'And I've never given you this,' said Myles. He handed Watts a printout of arrival times and transactions and interactions with the staff.

'Can I see them on CCTV?'

'You'll get me sacked.'

'We're safe as houses, Michael,' said Watts. He repositioned himself next to the hotel manager to view multiple screens at once. They started with bearded Owen Chard's Wednesday 11am arrival. He was accompanied by a woman, her face hidden by a beanie hat. Watts asked for emailed close ups of their faces. 'Who's the girl?'

'Chard's wife. Signed in as Becky Letts, her stage name apparently. Same Hare and Hounds address as his in Edinburgh. According to the duty log, her real name is Angelina Kozar, a Ukrainian who wants to be an actress. They had a fight before he kicked the bucket. She's pregnant too.'

'You got an outside view, showing them arriving?' asked Watts. Michael called up timed camera views covering the entrance to the hotel. They watched a black Golf arrive. Owen got out of the passenger seat, sat down on a chair outside the hotel and waited as the driver disappeared. They freeze-framed the image and Watts wrote down the numberplate. Last year's model. Not much change from twenty-five grand. A few minutes later, Owen's companion was back, carrying her rucksack with the beanie hat pulled tight over her head. 'Where is she likely to park?'

'There's a car park out back. Guests get a discount,' said Myles.

'OK. Next,' said Watts.

'Ed Boucher booking in at 3pm Wednesday.'

Watts watched the strutting peacock at the reception desk. He asked for a close-up and noted the perfect pencil-thin moustache. 'Next.' A couple of hours later Boucher was buying a gin and tonic. A red-headed woman in a little black cocktail dress joined him. More screen-grabs were taken. Watts had already sussed what was going on but wanted real evidence that could be used in court to back his gut. They watched Boucher and the little black dress, fast forwarding the boring bits and slowing down when the one-nighters ordered champagne. 'How many bottles?'

'Three.' The hotel manager almost skated over Boucher pouring the contents of a small bottle into the champagne glass, but Watts didn't miss it. He asked Myles to change to the CCTV covering the ladies' toilet. Becky watched Boucher spike the bubbly, rejoined him and swapped the glasses — a transition that bypassed Boucher, but not Watts. The next interaction was Becky's call to the reception to say that Owen Chard was dead. Next morning at breakfast, Myles screen-grabbed Becky and a different Boucher eating together. That was the man Watts had met earlier. The two Eds were like chalk and cheese. One posh. The other acting posh. One a natural born knob, the other a big-mouthed fake. Both had wanted to sting John Budd's trust fund for a quarter of a million pounds. 'Have you found what you're looking for?' asked Myles.

'Yes and no. Thanks for your time and patience. I've not been here. One more thing, who took the body?'

'The Co-op in Crumpsall.'

Watts found a corner in the coffee shop next door and called Carol Cox. He asked her to text the name of Owen Chard's agent, the locum doctor who had signed off Owen Chard's death and the contact details of Manchester's most prominent Ukrainian refugee champion. While he waited for her to respond, he checked Boucher, Chard, Letts and Kozar on the national crime register. Boucher was clean, not even a speeding ticket. Chard had traffic fines and cautions for drunk and disorderly, assaulting photographers, and domestics with his ex-wife. Becky Letts and Angelina Kozar didn't exist on any UK police databases. Watts ran the car number plate and came up with Jason and Jessica Long. They lived in Whitefield, not far from the Budds. He ran them through another database. Although they had drug and soliciting history in Sheffield, they were clean in Manchester.

Within a quarter of an hour Carol Cox answered his requests and he was back on the phone.

Owen Chard's agent, Charlie Wolff, picked up second ring with a jovial elongated hello. 'Apologies, I'm a police officer, ringing about Owen Chard who passed away in Manchester? I need your most recent pictures, preferably with and without the beard,' said Watts. 'What was he like, this Owen Chard?"

Wolff's tone flattened and he became more serious. 'A bit of a rogue, a Jack the Lad, a throwback to the last century. Owen held grudges against the character that made his name and his hard-working agent. All the work I did for him for free and he sacks me from beyond the grave. Well, his wife did.'

'Recent photographs?'

'You know, he hated Billy Whyte. Didn't think the character was a proper acting role. He forgot they merely asked him to play himself, like they do with all soap opera stars. They work too hard and too fast to actually act. Learn the lines, stand on the spot marked X, deliver them. Next scene, repeat ad infinitum,' said Charlie.

'Did you know his wife?'

'Not his new one. Never heard of her before. Never knew he was getting spliced. Always was a sucker for a pretty face.'

'Did he have a bad heart?'

'Owen? Fit as a butcher's dog,' said Charlie.

'Thanks for your time,' said Watts. An up-to-date image pinged into his mobile inbox. Watts dictated notes into his mobile. He called Doctor Norma Jones to discuss the previous night. She said Chard was fitted with a pacemaker. Only a matter of time, if she was speaking off the record. The cause of Chard's death wasn't sudden, violent or unnatural such as an accident, or suicide. It was down to the coroner's office to decide what to do next, no skin off her nose. The doctor had signed off too many deaths to get hung up on one.

It was late and had been a long day. Watts left the hotel and walked around the corner from the hotel to the NCP car park and entered. He found the VW black Golf in a cramped ground floor space. He checked the doors. They were locked. He peered through the tinted windows. The rear passenger seats were dotted with hotel and restaurant receipts from different northern cities. Why had they stupidly kept evidence that could be used against them? Watts took some photographs. He would arrange for the hotels to be called tomorrow. He spotted a tee on to the back seat with words on the front … 'CU'. He could guess the rest. He dictated more notes on his mobile. They were opportunists, semi-professional grifters, out of their depth. He could call their bluff any time, but he needed real evidence for the CPS if they were going to do time. He was tired and would kill for a quiet reflective pint before he went home.

Thirty-one

There would be plenty of time for reflection and a pint when Watts retired and he found himself invisible, defined by the number of annual foreign holidays he and Frankie took. Rather than supping a cool pint of bitter with a frothy head, Watts walked to King's Street. He stopped in front of an office above SharkBite, an independent fashion retailer specialising in surfer accessories, even though the nearest beach was ninety minutes away. A light was on. A woman was working. He was not the only mug clocking up unpaid overtime at 10.30pm. Watts called and saw the woman above answer instantly.

'Nina Mazur. How can I help?'

'My name's Detective Inspector Nigel Watts. I'm looking for an Angelina Kozar. Are you free for a chat?'

'At this hour?'

'I'm outside,' said Watts. Thirty seconds later, Nina welcomed Watts into her office. He apologised for the late call and explained that he needed background. Nina said she was a lawyer who had lived in England for twenty years and was not sure how she could help. Her pro bono work with Ukrainian refugees was confidential and took up most of her free time, but she still had to make a living. Nina said she couldn't break the trust of her clients. Watts held up his hands. Said he understood her position, but what could she tell him about Angelina Kozar?

'Why are you interested in her?'

'She's a witness to a sudden death. Just want to confirm her identity.' Nigel showed her two stills on his mobile. One with the beanie on her head. The other dressed in the little black number. 'Are they both her?'

Nina nodded. 'Yes. Is she in trouble? She had a bad time with the Russians.'

'Where?'

'Bucha.'

'How bad is bad?'

'You would need to ask her directly, I'm afraid. I'll tell her you were asking after her. Do you have a business card with your details that I can give her?'

'Not on me.'

'A number I can give her?' asked Nina.

'It's the one on your mobile when I just called you. What's she like?' asked Watts.

'Before the invasion or now?'

'Either.'

'Imagine your worst nightmare and treble it,' said Nina.

'Can you tell me about it?'

'Watch the news. Read the newspapers. It's too late and I'm too tired to give you a lesson on the horrors of Russia's brutality.'

'If you speak to her, tell her she's not in any trouble,' said Watts.

'OK,' said Nina.

Watts thanked Nina for her time, apologised again for the lateness of the visit and drove across town to the Co-op undertakers to identify the stiff on ice. On the way, he called an old friend to do a spot of unpaid overtime.

Old Tosh, the morgue assistant, stared blankly at the body tagged as Owen Chard. Tosh was a traumatised Falklands vet. Occasionally he talked about the cost of capturing Mount Longdon with 2 Para. Clearing bodies from the battleground, his mates worried people might think they were gay if a dead soldier's trousers fell down when they were being moved. That ignorance made an impression and when he left the Paras he went to work for a funeral director for the summer and stayed.

Watts snapped Boucher's head alongside a photograph of Chard. There was, as he fully expected, absolutely no ambiguity.

'Death is the great equaliser,' said Old Tosh. 'I'll have worked here forty years in October. They keep offering to retire me, but how would I kill my spare time?'

'What happens if the bodies get mixed up?' asked Watts.

'Nothing, if nobody notices. Why make the bereavement worse?'

'Easily done then?'

'You want me to lose the man who isn't Owen Chard for you?'

'Why would I want to do that?' Watts asked

'I don't know. I'm not a detective,' replied Old Tosh.

'If …' Watts stopped himself.

'You're too honest a man, Nigel Watts. My tired eyes see nothing. Macular degeneration. I have injections. Shout if you want me to make a mistake. My advice, don't corrupt yourself.'

Watts had enough evidence for the CPS to prosecute Chard for not reporting a death, impersonating a dead man and attempted blackmail. Chard's defence team would play the 'John Budd' card. The joker in the pack. Once in an open court, John Budd's reputation was ruined forever.

Outside the funeral parlour, Watts posted a 24-hour Code 66 to help out a trusted colleague. Watts would ask the pro bono detectives who turned up to rewind the movements of everyone involved in the blackmail plot. Once he understood the blackmailers' motivations, he could make a counteroffer.

Finally, Watts visited tech genius Cassie Holmes. She lived in Radcliffe. He wanted to step into John Budd's digital footprint. He apologised for calling at silly o'clock when she had young kids but said he needed a strictly confidential digital sweep on Big John's electronic devices. He told her he'd pop back in the morning and left the devices with her to download overnight.

Watts drove around Manchester for an hour, unable to unwind and knowing his beloved Frankie would spot he was stressing.

When Watts finally got home, Frankie was fast asleep. She always insisted on a good eight hours' uninterrupted sleep.

He went back downstairs and transcribed the Budd abuse letter. He printed it out. Did the writer have inside info? John using 'Nigel' as an alias, the tattoos on his bum, the boomerang penis. The only mistake was the anal sex. Watts and Budd had gone into the bedroom of a male student violently raped by an older man. The victim's bed and duvet were covered in shit and blood, and Budd had been sick. He was too revolted to joke about it afterwards, called in the devil's dirty old canal. He said Heather wanted him to navigate up there for a change, but he always thought it was no different from boning a bloke. Now Heather had confirmed JB's anal aversion, Watts knew the letter was highly suspect and everything collapsed like a house of cards. He'd get the proof and then kick their butts all the way to the Crown Court — and make sure John Budd's name was never mentioned, to boot.

Friday 10th June 2022
Thirty-two

Occasional splashes hit Owen's face. The drops rolled into his closed eyelids and pooled. He wasn't sure if he was still dreaming or half awake. Owen opened his eyes. A red liquid film blurred his vision. He tried to rub his eyes to restore his sight, but his arms and shoulders were pinned to the bed, like Becky had bound Ed Boucher to the four poster the night he died. Bits of yesterday evening returned. He'd been chatting to Alice, Boucher's co-conspirator, thinking he was in control. Keep your friends close and your enemies closer.

That strategy had backfired.

Alice was sitting naked on his chest, her knees pressed down on his shoulders and upper arms. Her left arm was held vertically over his face and her elbow almost touched his nose. She squeezed her hand and blood ran from a cut and splashed on him. 'What's going on?'

'Cutting myself for the last time. Celebrating my freedom. I used to feel better when I bled.' Alice's exposed multi-pierced vulva was inches from his mouth. If Owen ever found it hard to sleep, he could always count her studs, not that the time was right for wisecracking. 'Another ride?' asked Alice. She leant back, gripped his semi-tumescence, and yanked it like a joystick. Owen was at the mercy of an insane self-harmer. She could kill him any time she

103

wanted. His second obituary would read, the falling, failing actor who died twice.

'Don't do anything silly,' said Owen.

'I'm joking with you, Owen. Pulling your plonker, literally,' said Alice. She rolled off him, put the knife on the bedside table and stood up. She went to the toilet, leaving the door open. They could still see each other, like an old married couple.

'What are you doing here?'

'Discussing blackmailing John Budd's healthcare fund for twenty-five thousand pounds with you,' said Alice.

'How much do you want?' said Owen. He realised Becky had misheard the amount Boucher wanted. They'd asked for ten times the original figure.

'Discussing money is so vulgar,' said Alice. 'Where's the creativity in money?'

'Depends how hungry you are,' said Owen.

Alice wiped herself. It was his turn to relieve himself. He peed, thought how no one ever got caught short on TV, flushed the loo and walked back into the room. She was half dressed, cleaning the wound on her arm, covering it with a dressing and a bandage. 'Come here and sit next to me. Pretend we're at the cinema,' said Alice.

Owen did as he was told and pulled on his boxers. Alice picked up Ed's mobile and played a video. Owen watched Angelina interrogate Ed about rape. 'Was he a rapist? Did he …with you?'

'She let Ed die.'

'She tried to restart his heart,' said Owen.

'Let's watch another video, last night's highlights.'

Owen viewed himself undressed and comatose on the bed. Alice's filming fluctuated between her talking directly to the camera and showing off his body. 'This is Owen Chard, who faked his own death so he could impersonate my granddad. Hunky beast isn't he? Nice member. A good size. Almost as big as his ego. Shall I put the beast inside me?' Owen watched her slap him awake. There was non-consensual sexual intercourse. Alice rode him cowgirl. After a minute she climbed off. 'Not a bad ride, but not as good as cutting yourself to escape the emptiness.' Alice cut her arm with the blade and stopped filming.

"What do you want from me?' asked Owen.

'I want to feel real,' said Alice. 'That's why I'm doing the writing MA. They can teach me to feel. I'm emotionally numb. Even Ed's death doesn't move me. Can you help me, Owen? That song you wrote. Sorry, I Made You Cry When I Almost Died. The sentiments resonate with me. Make me feel you understand me. I'll sing it to you.'

In the cold, bleak night, I nearly slipped away,
Fading in the shadows, where darkness held its sway,
I saw your face, so pale, so wide-eyed,
Sorry I made you cry when I almost died.

But the world is a fractured, desolate place,
And I couldn't keep up with its relentless pace,
In the void, I found solace, but it cost us, I decide,
Sorry I made you cry when I almost died.

In the ghostly echoes of Joy Division's primitive sound,
A needle and a spoon made me sound profound,
Our friend, Ian Curtis, was our haunting guide,
Sorry I made you cry when I almost died.

The pulsing rhythms of life almost slipped away,
In the footsteps of darkness, I felt I couldn't stay,
I know my absence will leave you shattered inside,
Sorry I made you cry when I almost died.

Songwriters: Owen Chard/Caroline Bell/Angus Ian

Please don't, thought Owen. But it was too late. He was lost for words, didn't know whether to laugh or cry. Alice beat her chest to keep time. Owen clapped when she finished and she smiled back. He hoped she wasn't going to sing Flat Earth. Owen told Alice Sorry was a simple pop song written in half an hour. Caroline got a credit because she used the title line when she came around after an overdose. It wasn't a design for life. Just words that rhymed.

'A sad song says so much to me,' said Alice.

It's just a ditty, thought Owen. Did people really think they could learn more from a three-minute record than they ever learned from school, to paraphrase Springsteen? Ironically, his ex-wife Caroline could help Alice. She was a mental health nurse. But she wasn't here, he was. He had to keep her on side and happy. He would say whatever it took to keep him alive. 'What happens next?' asked Owen.

'We write a song. Start a screenplay. The twenty-five grand can fund our creativity,' replied Alice. 'Where do we begin?'

'A title is a good place. Get a good title and you have the start of your chorus or a catchy refrain you can repeat.'

'That easy?'

'In theory.' Owen checked Ed's mobile. No calls yet, the chief constable was maintaining radio silence. Alice flopped on the bed, a snow angel, her left hand in Owen's lap.

'I'm exhausted,' said Alice.

'You want to hear something funny?' asked Owen.

'What?'

'Becky misheard Ed when he talked about the blackmail cash. She thought he said two hundred and fifty thousand pounds. That's what I asked for,' said Owen.

Alice smiled a huge cheesecake grin and fist-bumped Owen. 'We can do even more with a quarter of a million,' said Alice.

'Creativity was never about the money. More like getting demons off your chest,' said Owen. 'What are your demons?'

'Will putting them in a song make them go away?'

'Helped me once. I joke about the creative process. Self-deprecation is such an English thing. What would you write about?'

'My mum vanishing in front of me at a railway station and how I was blamed by people who were meant to love me.'

'That's heavy duty,' said Owen.

'Not really. You become numb to feelings. Only way to feel anything is to cut yourself or hurt somebody else really bad. Does that make me radio rental?'

'No. Confused. You were a child. You had to trust the adults,' said Owen. One thing was for certain, she was volatile, like undiluted nitroglycerin. She had to be handled with extreme care or she was in danger of blowing everything up, including herself.

'Could be a song. Showing two perspectives of my mother's death. One where she jumps and the other where she's pushed,' said Alice. 'Both could be true. Both could be false. She could have slipped.'

'Here's a song title for you, *Ambiguity Blues*. A narrative song. Tells a story,' said Owen. Songwriting takes you to some dark places if you aren't careful, exposes you as vulnerable. That's why a lot of songwriters simply made shit up. Bruce Springsteen said his early songs were fake, created in his imagination, not grounded in reality. Robbie Williams lied about who penned *Angels*. The song was half written by a drunken Dubliner who was erased from the copyright record. Ruined the song for him and Robbie's nice guy image.

'You're the first person I've ever told how my mother might have died,' said Alice.

'Which version is fact?' asked Owen.

'I don't know,' said Alice. 'It's like catching water in a net.' That's a great song title, Catching Water in a Net. Will you help me write the rest of it? Mentor me?'

Thirty-three

The off-duty detectives arrived in the McDonald's car park between six and quarter past in the morning. They parked in the furthest corner, away from the A56 that linked Bury and Manchester. They popped into the fast-food restaurant for coffees and breakfast meal deals. Watts walked among his colleagues. They had taken a day off, pulled a sickie or said they were working from home. He thanked them for attending and said what was discussed should never be shared beyond the group. No media leaks or beer gossip or pillow talk, everything was off-the-record. Anyone uncomfortable could drive away.

Each detective nodded consent.

Watts was going to openly disobey his orders from Hurst and Cabinet Office rules about discussing pending awards. He explained that John Budd was in line for a George Cross, but a London nominations assessor questioned JB's credibility. His name was Ed Boucher. Watts wanted background on him and his family and two other players — the recently deceased actor Owen Chard and a Ukrainian refugee, Angelina Kozar alias Becky Letts. They were potentially carrying out a honey-trapping scam in the north of England and drove a black VW Golf. He gave them the registration and told them where it could be found. He wanted to know where the motor had been. 'Forget honey-trapping prosecution. We're after intelligence to ensure

John gets his cross. We don't want any misunderstandings for the media to get their knickers in a twist. Any questions?'

There were none.

Watts split them into teams of four, one for Boucher, one for Chard, one for Kozar, and the fourth to track the car. He told them he'd already spoken to Nina Mazur at the Ukrainian Refugee Centre in Manchester. Kozar was pregnant and traumatised, a victim of Russian war crimes in Ukraine. They would meet at seven in the evening at the Eagle and Child pub near the golf course. He'd have a word with the landlord about a private room and a tab for the debrief.

By seven thirty they had all left the car park. That was the easy part. Now he had the unenviable task of checking how corrupt his best friend was.

He drove to Radcliffe and knocked on the door. Cassie Holmes greeted him. The kids and hubby were in full riot mode and they left them to it downstairs. She closed the attic studio door which doubled as music studio for her guitarist husband. Her husband had brewed coffee and left four chocolate biscuits. 'We rely on my wages. His money is inconsistent,' said Cassie.

'What've you found?'

'What day was John hurt?'

'Friday 25th June 2021.'

'He wasn't wearing his Fitbit,' said Cassie.

'Forgot to put it on?'

'He always monitored himself. Didn't use his phone either.' Watts had seen John use a mobile phone throughout Friday. A burner phone was the obvious answer. How come nobody had spotted these anomalies? Simple, no one had looked. Big John was above suspicion, his catastrophic injuries ruled out his culpability. Watts grimaced at their collective complacency. 'He's also a compulsive gambler,' said Cassie.

Watts had heard it so many times, criminals justifying themselves. They slipped into illegal activities by accident, debts spiralled out of control. He and John liked a sporting bet — a tenner here, twenty there, nothing serious. 'Online?'

'RedORBlack and Sunshine.' She said the passwords were saved and double-clicked admission codes had been sent to Budd's mobile on the desk beside her. She had access and they looked at the two accounts. John was busy — and unsuccessful. He carried big debts, until he correctly called the Juke and Muller bout a draw at fifteen to one. Staked ten grand at RedORBlack and two grand at Sunshine. His gambling debts cleared and a ninety grand balance untouched. A cynic would say a boxing insider tipped John off about the fix. Only one name sprang to his mind, mutual friend Harry Quinn, JJ's trainer. 'Can you search for Harry Quinn in John's emails?' asked Watts.

Cassie clicked the mouse and whizzed around the screen. Watts hoped nothing would come up. 'Nothing for Harry, but a Shannon Quinn contacted John the week before he was hurt.'

'What does she say?'

'FYI,' said Holmes. 'And a picture of herself braless in a crop top and tight cut-off jeans in front of her cab.'

'Anything else?' Watts looked at the screen. Was John shagging Shannon? The signature had the details of her black cab business with email, website, mobile and social media accounts and contact details.

'Just a reply, saying "Ta" with a couple of kisses,' Holmes replied.

Watts checked his own mobile. There was a presser at the Manchester Arena this afternoon. Wherever JJ roamed, Harry Quinn would be in his shadow. Watts would pay them a visit. He needed to book a taxi. Cassie understood and read out Shannon's number. Watts called and arranged for a pick-up. He felt nervous, worried about what he was going to find out. His gut instincts made him feel very uncomfortable.

Thirty-four

Angelina wanted to talk rape, death and war crimes. Nina wanted to explain why a termination was wrong in God's eyes. Angelina wanted to eat her breakfast. Nina said adoption was an option if she wasn't able to bring up a child by herself. Angelina said it was her choice as a woman and nobody should interfere. Nina said the foetus was already taking shape in her belly after nearly fourteen weeks. Angelina said bringing an unwanted, unloved child into the world was a crime against humanity. She needed support, not condemnation. The dark places had been darker than anyone could imagine. Nina apologised.

They went to the King's Street office suite, where Elina set up the video camera. They would tape everything. Elina would reference the digital images. Nina said Angelina should use her own words, no matter how graphic or revolting. There would be no prompts for lawyers to claim she was coached if they ever got to a war crimes court. Angelina cleared her throat. She was talking to two friends in a room where cartoon animals roamed wild on the wall. She was also talking to the world, and to loved ones who soared beyond the great divide between life and infinity.

My name is Angelina Kozar. I am 27 years old. I was born in Kyiv on 24th

January, 1997. I am an orphan. I grew up in Odessa with my aunt. My mother died in a car crash when I was ten. My father, I never knew. My mother never said anything about him. He may still be alive. But he does not count. He was never there. Either through choice or ignorance. My mother travelled and worked in Liverpool, Manchester and Leeds in the mid-nineties, so my father might not be a Ukrainian or even know I exist.

I trained as a nurse in Kyiv. I met Marko at the hospital where he was training to be a doctor. We worked on an A&E shift and fell in love. A whirlwind romance was followed by a long engagement until we could secure our future together. We wed as soon as he qualified and had the money to build a life together. We wanted to start a family and have children before the end of our twenties, two of each was our dream. We bought a house in Bucha, twenty miles from the capital where we worked. Marko had lived there all his life with his brother Borden and cousin Symon. We didn't want to mix work and our personal lives 24/7. I quit nursing and became a journalist. Specialised in healthcare and social services.

We had to put our plans on hold. Although there was talk about a Russian invasion, nobody believed it was real. We said the diplomats would make Putin see sense. When we heard the first explosions, we hoped it was fireworks, but we all knew the Russians were trying to terrify us into immediate submission. Shellshocked, we didn't have a clue what to do. Forty thousand people lived in Bucha and 90 per cent left immediately. Those who stayed were too frail, sick or stubborn to leave their homes. We stayed. On Sunday, 27th February an invader's convoy was gridlocked in Station Street. After the first vehicle was hit, Ukrainian artillery picked them off one by one as they panicked and retreated. In response, the Russians said civilians were the enemy too.

After bloody Sunday, the Russians started indiscriminately exterminating Ukrainians. Nobody was safe. They parked their tanks in private houses. Looted whatever they wanted. Drinks, televisions, even bloody underwear. Hijacked cars. Raced them around town. Then crushed them with their tanks. Our electricity, water and gas were cut off. We had to get water from wells. Every time you stepped outside, you risked being killed. I witnessed dozens of deaths. A surgeon who worked with Marko, his wife and their four-year-old daughter were murdered in airstrikes. Five men in the next street were executed by Russians. Hands tied behind their backs. Bullets in the back of their heads. A construction worker was shot walking up his stairs and then blown up by a grenade. A small convoy of cars was attacked, another father and daughter murdered by Russian soldiers. Me and Marko would skirt around town tending to the injured. Borden and Symon distributed food and water to our neighbours and friends. We ran like rabbits around the town. Hid like rats. Although we stayed one step ahead of the Russians, we knew our luck would run out.

At the end of March, they came for us. Half a dozen soldiers. We were cooking borscht when they burst in. They thought we were all men. My height and my clothing, designed to keep me warm, didn't distinguish me from the others. My hair under a hat. No make-up. They took us to a basement cellar at a school. Tied our hands behind our backs. Held guns to our heads. Carried out mock executions. Fired questions at us about the whereabouts of Zelensky, our troops and civilian spies. Two soldiers watched over us. Others cooked and drank in the playground outside the school basement. We talked about escaping. The boys said I should go. I refused to leave them. The guards let us use a corner of the basement to relieve ourselves, one at a time. I went last, hoping they wouldn't notice me squatting. A third soldier had entered the basement, armed with an assault rifle and a pistol. He was dressed differently to the other guards. I finished and was pulling up my trousers when he called me over to him and instructed me to follow out of the basement into the school. He guided me to a classroom on the top floor. Said the higher we climbed, the hornier he felt.

Once inside, he pointed his pistol at me. Ordered me to undress or he would shoot me in the face. He told me to give him oral sex. Held the gun to my temple. Fired twice at the ceiling to motivate me to work harder. Then he raped me. Afterwards, he let me put on a top because it was so cold. Said I could sit down on a chair. He produced a packet of cigarettes. Shared one with me. We blew smoke rings and played with them like teenagers. He had a knife. Glided the tip over my face. My legs. My neck. Nicked me a few of times. Slapped me lots. Pulled my hair. Choked me. Smoked more cigarettes and demanded more oral sex before he raped me for a second time. Waved the gun in my face. Told me to suck the barrel. Then he gave me oral. Made me kiss him like a girlfriend. Said I reminded him of his sisters and his aunty. Told me his name was Andrei Orlov. Said I should always remember his name because he had saved my life. Half an hour later I heard three shots in succession, followed by another three. We sat there. Chain smoked more cigarettes. Finally, he led me out the back way to avoid the other Russian soldiers. Said I should run west. I ran and never said goodbye to Marko, Symon and Borden. I deserted them. Every step I ran was a humiliation. Until today. Thank you for listening. And crying with me. I am not alone anymore.

Angelina asked if she was wrong. Was it a mistake to have taken a rapist's word that her husband, his brother and his cousin were dead. Had she run from Ukraine for no reason?

'They were identified where you said they were. They have been buried together,' said Nina. She wiped tears from her eyes.

Angelina said she would show her videos and photographs in reverse order. She used one of Nina's MacBook Pro laptops to enter her cloud account. Elina took notes and referenced each image and video. Angelina explained the story behind each one.

Ten hours had flown by, the women lost in time. When they finished, Angelina made a short speech to the two exhausted women.

'There are two reasons I want an abortion. First, I know who the father is who has invaded my womb without permission. Second, I believe the same thing happened to my mother in England.'

'Jesus,' said Nina. 'I am so sorry.'

Manchester had so much to answer for, thought Angelina. Somewhere in the city her father was going about his business oblivious, but her mother never shared her good news with him. Angelina said she dreaded having the baby and Andrei Orlov turning up in the future and claiming parental rights.

'He won't be doing that in this world,' said Elina. 'I've searched dead Russian soldiers online. Do you want to see the picture?'

There was a blurry photograph. A dead Russian soldier. Alone on a road next to a burned-out military vehicle. Angelina recognised Andrei Orlov's uniform. Half his face had started to bloat. The other half was missing.

'When?'

'A week after he left Bucha.'

Was Angelina relieved? Neither Elina nor Nina said a word. There were no words. His death would not change her mind about the abortion.

Thirty-five

What did Alice want from him, beyond writing imaginary songs and screenplays? A full English breakfast, apparently. The works, grilled Cumberland sausage, sweet-cured bacon, black pudding, baked tomato, mushrooms, potato croquettes and poached eggs. She said shagging all night made her ravenous and stuffed half a grilled sausage in her mouth without any hint of irony. He picked Eggs Benedict, toasted English muffin, soft poached eggs, Hollandaise sauce and smoked salmon.

'What are you going to do today?' Alice asked, as if yesterday had never happened and tomorrow was never going to arrive.

'Waiting for the chief to call me,' replied Owen.

'Aren't you booked into see the neurosurgeon and the newspaper editor?'

Owen looked at Boucher's mobile and checked the iCal app. He was meant to be seeing Helen Tapody at eleven and Jane Church at two. 'Yes. I'll cancel by email,' said Owen.

'Don't you dare. After you've seen them, they'll call the chief. You've got to carry on planting seeds,' said Alice.

'What are you going to do?'

'I'll come with you. Sit in reception. Plan songs and our screenplay.'

Two hours later Owen was sitting in front of Helen Tapody, feigning interest about John Budd's medical history. Tapody said John Budd broke both his legs in multiple places, his pelvis, his ankle, five ribs and fractured his skull. John also suffered damage to his kidneys, and his spleen was removed. His heart stopped twice on the way to the hospital. Since then, Budd's bones had healed but he was unable to communicate or look after himself. He needed 24-hour specialist care and had no memory of who he had been and was. He was at constant risk of infections, which could be fatal.

'Will he get better?' asked Owen.

'We had a case back in Australia where a coma victim had forgotten everything. When he woke up, his attention span was minimal, and his IQ test was the lowest score possible. No one gave him a chance, apart from a young therapist who refused to give up on him. After only two years, he went from being practically helpless to living on his own with only minor assistance,' said Tapody.

'Who was the therapist?'

'Me. I was a part-time therapist at medical school. It paid my fees. And I married the patient. Sadly, he died of cancer several years ago when we lived in Oslo. Our dream was to buy an island in the sun.'

'I am sorry to hear about your husband. And are you going to do the same for John Budd?' asked Owen.

'Yes. He's got all the money he needs to support his rehab, and my team are working really hard with him several times a week,' said Tapody.

'He has a bright future?'

'And a George Cross. I know it's supposed to be a secret, but I'm so excited. Sir Richard let the cat out of the bag.'

'Meant to be confidential. I'm here doing due diligence. Don't want to embarrass HRH,' said Owen.

'I've heard.'

'From the chief.'

'Anyone can write a letter and make allegations. If you're a betting man, I'd put a fiver on John walking unaided again. I know John would bet on himself,' said Tapody. Owen smiled. Was Helen a little in love with her patient, blinding herself to the bleeding obvious?

Later, Owen was sitting in the editor's office at the Manchester Daily

News. The editor Jane Church was busy on her computer. She apologised, saying they were short staffed. There was no money in printed newspapers, they had to give it away. The advertising had dried up. On the plus side, they weren't pulping forests anymore.

Owen inspected framed newspaper covers showcasing Manchester's history. Alongside positive stories celebrating the city, there were darker headlines: Strangeways riots, IRA bombs, serial killer Harold Shipman, Stephen Oake murdered arresting a terrorist, two female police officers killed by Dale Cregan, Paul Massey's gangland shooting, a homegrown bomber in the Manchester Arena killing 22 young people at an Ariana Grande concert and a chief constable resigning because the police force failed to record a fifth of all crimes. 'That's quite a collection,' Owen said.

Church looked up from her computer. 'Manchester has a violent history. I covered a lot of the crime stories as a senior and then a chief reporter. Imagine being a police officer attending a domestic and a nutter shoots you and chucks a hand grenade at you? Or a jobsworth enters your office with a bullshit story about John Budd and an alleged sexual assault?'

'I can't,' said Owen. The chief constable didn't understand the concept of 'private and confidential'. Didn't matter, as long as he got paid.

'We raised over one million pounds from public donations. Manchester demands a George Cross. Anything less is an insult to his sacrifice. Do you understand?'

'Yes,' said Owen.

'I'm not sure you do. As a trustee, we've discussed the alleged sexual abuse and I'm not buying it. How do you know she isn't lying? You weren't there,' said Church.

'Neither were you,' replied Owen.

'She should put her allegations to the test. You claim you're the messenger. Well act like one and tell her this sucks. She should ditch the anonymous victim card and go on the record. Aren't you ashamed?' asked Church.

'How long did it take for Stephen Oake to receive his posthumous Queen's Gallantry Medal?'

'Too long.'

'Too right. John Budd will have to wait an eternity.' Owen took his mobile out of his briefcase. 'I'll put you in touch with the Cabinet Office. Somebody will tell you what you can and cannot publish.'

'There's no need to be hasty, Mr Boucher. The chief's in charge, not me,' said Church.

Alice was waiting in the reception and jumped up when he reappeared. He debriefed her in the Uber. She said Church's reaction was perfect. 'This is great stuff. You can take the higher moral ground because he's broken your trust and compromised your request for confidentiality. He'll be squirming with embarrassment and won't be able to give you the diamonds quick enough.'

'Really? Hurst hasn't called,' said Owen.

'Patience. The deluded prick thinks he's in control when we hold all the aces,' said Alice. 'Have you had any ideas about songs?'

'I'll bow to your greater experience about the chief. How many times did Ed and you blackmail people?'

'That would be telling. Do you want a drug-free fuck?'

'No, Jodie,' said Owen.

'Who's Jodie?' asked Alice.

'Jodie Foster,' said Owen. 'Foster was 12 when she played teenage prostitute Iris in *Taxi Driver* alongside Robert De Niro. His 'You talkin' to me? You talkin' to me?' rap inspired Billy Whyte's 'You're talking to the wrong man'. Really applies now, more than ever.'

'You old men are so boring. Will there be lots of fucking in the movie we're going to make with Budd's money? What about a theme tune about talking to the wrong man?' asked Alice.

'Are you serious?' asked Owen.

'Deadly serious,' said Alice. 'Never underestimate me and my creativity.'

THIRTY-SIX

The licence badge on the perspex partition of the black cab said 'Shannon Quinn, number 887906'. Shannon's picture showed an unsmiling hard-nosed woman with her hair pulled back from her face. Watts looked at the driver's reflection in the rearview mirror. The image bore little resemblance to the reality. Shannon was all business on the ID mugshot. In reality, she was a Saturday Night Girl ready to walk over hot coals in bare feet to get to the next party. Watts' dear old mum would have called Shannon blousy with her upfront chest, heavy make up and peroxided hair. 'Where are we going? Manchester?' asked Shannon.

'Have you had lunch?' Watts replied.

'Been busy.'

'My treat. On the clock.'

'What's going on?'

'Join me in the back after we've got our food,' said Watts.

'Do I need a lawyer or a condom?'

'Very funny, have you done something wrong? Harry wouldn't like me boning his sister. Might end up with us being related. Let's eat,' said Watts. Shannon did as she was told. Drove through the McDonalds in Whitefield and purchased takeaway Big Mac meal deals with shakes. Watts paid cash.

She parked up in corner of the car park, partially hidden by overhanging trees. Turned off the engine and climbed in the back to join Watts. She undid the bun and let her hair fall over her face. 'Why are you doing that?'

'In case you change your mind about wanting to seduce me. I have a thing for old dicks with badges,' said Shannon.

'Mrs Watts would be wearing my testicles as earrings, tempting as it is.' No harm in playing the sex banter game if it loosened her tongue. He bit into his burger, let the sauces smudge over his chin. She did the same. 'Never knew you were a black cab driver.' Watts took another couple of bites and the burger was gone. He started on the chips. They tasted good dipped in the BBQ sauce. Shannon shared his sachet. Poked her own chips into the sweet brown ming. Chips gone, they sucked on the straws. Sipped cold chocolate milkshake.

'With three kids to feed, needs must. Better than the alternative, working in a massage parlour. Thankfully they're at their gran's this weekend. She's got a cottage in the Lakes. Hates it when Harry is in fight mode,' said Shannon.

'Their dad contributes?' asked Watts.

'Plural. Three kids. Three dads. They give me sweet FA. Hard to find a good man and keep him alive or out of jail. They promise so much to get in your knickers and deliver so little. Number four is on the way and the father is younger and full of promises.'

'Congratulations on the baby … and fingers crossed for the father,' said Watts.

'Cut the crap. What do you want, Nigel?'

'What you say in this cab, stays in this cab,' said Watts. 'This is an unofficial friendly chat. It will never be used in evidence, but you must talk to me NOW.'

'We're not in a movie, Nigel.'

'It's the anniversary of the death of your eldest this weekend.'

'And your mate being crippled.'

'Anything on your conscience?' Watts had been at the station when Shannon arrived to identify her son. The reception was packed with belligerent officers. They had come to donate blood, carry out an inch-by-inch search of the crime scene. Shannon walked in by herself, shaking with grief. Nobody wanted to tell her that her son had been burned to a cinder and was unrecognisable. Watts volunteered, and held Shannon when she broke into bits. He looked over her shoulder at the contempt on the faces of his fellow officers and he accompanied her to the hospital. She constantly said it was her fault and he didn't understand at the time. He had a better idea now.

'Like what?'

'You tell me. Must be hard to live with,' said Watts.

'The death of my son? Yes, it is. Very hard,' said Shannon. 'What do you want from me?'

'Were you having an affair with John Budd?'

Shannon hissed with laughter. Sucked through her teeth. Nibbled at the straw still in her mouth. 'Me? Fucking John?'

'Yes.'

'He was too busy gambling to spend his time fucking my arse.'

'I know all about John and his involvement in the kidnapping,' said Watts, taking a punt on Shannon thinking he knew more than did. The guilty often thought talking about the nightmares that kept them awake at night would lighten the heavy load.

'That's a relief. John said you'd met a couple of rich mugs. Once in a lifetime opportunity, but he had to act fast. He wanted to rob them to pay off his debts. His plan was simple. He'd separate the couple and abduct the wife, with the husband handing over their gold watches and jewellery. Or rob them at gunpoint in the room. The whole thing would take an hour, tops,' said Shannon. 'Obviously, he needed help dead quick. Asked my Paul and my nephew Stevie to do their crazy Salford hoodlum routine. He knew them both from Harry's gym. A third man would do the collecting. Paul couldn't find a third man because all his mates were at a stag party, so he asked me because it was such short notice. We agreed a grand, a fifth of what Budd's little helpers were going to get.'

'And you took it?' asked Watts, realising the entire Greater Manchester police force and the Independent Office for Police Conduct had missed the bleeding obvious. 'You're the third "man"?'

'A grand is a grand. Upfront. Pays for a lot of schooling. John managed to convince the wife to grab a black cab on the pretext of doing some last-minute shopping. John had given Paul a gun loaded with blanks to scare everyone.'

'What went wrong?'

'Paul lost his head and cut the rings off the wife's finger,' said Shannon. 'I heard them fighting over the WhatsApp chat.'

Watts knew the missing finger had never been made public. A false confession filter. Shannon knew about it. Either she was there like she claimed, or somebody had told her about the amputation. 'And?'

'John knew if he walked away from this without a scratch, things get suspicious. He's telling me where he is, telling me to run him down and don't hold back on the revs,' said Shannon.

'A bit of improvisation ruined a man and his family?'

'If you say so. I was only meant to collect the diamonds, jewellery and gold from the hotel. That's why they paid me less, although I never saw any money. I take the cab to the lock up. Go home, sit down and wait. Watch everything unfold on the news in floods of tears,' said Shannon.

'And I consoled you and didn't understand what you meant when you said it was your fault,' said Watts.

'I always laugh when the police said they were looking for a third man. Not that funny, is it?'

Wasn't funny at all. She cried and he gave her the clean hanky he always carried around with him for impromptu confessions. They always played out the same. Remorse, self-pity and tears. Always lots of crying and sobbing. Then they had to write it down and do it all again and get them to sign their version of events that they may rely on in court. They always missed that bit on the telly and in crime books. The administration never made for exciting viewing or reading. 'You told anyone else?' asked Watts.

'Just my older brother, Harry.'

'What did he say?'

'He told me never to confess. Or tell anyone else. Lovers and sons and you included.'

'That's even better advice. Stick to it. If in doubt, say nowt,' said Watts, unable to stop the platitudes rolling off his tongue. She was already doing time. Her sentence would never end. What did she expect? She had crossed the sandy line between good and bad, joined the damned. Unlike the suicide club, the group didn't constantly need new members, but once you signed up, you could never leave. 'What happened to Zara's rings and her finger?'

'I presume John had them,' Shannon replied.

Watts checked the hanky for wet tears. There weren't any. Smudged black mascara, plenty. Crocodile tears, no. At face value, he had the third 'man', but it was very convenient. There was a reason cynics made good detectives.

Thirty-seven

The press conference was packed, with standing room only. Watts flashed his ID badge and said he was here to see Harry Quinn. A security guard who boxed at Harry's gym let him enter after inspecting his badge longer than necessary.

Watts walked into the large conference room. A huge, branded stage was the focus of journalists, photographers and broadcast crews. Half a dozen logos were splashed on the backdrop, with Baltic Power the most prominent icon. On the top table, promoter Salim Abo separated the two boxing camps. On his left was Juke, flanked by Harry Quinn. On the right, Wolfgang Muller, and his father and trainer, Sepp Muller. Behind them, the chief constable was standing with Zara Abo. Salim said he was looking forward to the highest grossing world heavyweight title fight and the values of the east and west aligning under one red sun. The chief spotted Watts and nodded in his direction. Zara followed the chief's eyes and blanked him. Neither Salim nor Zara had been in touch since the incident. Samantha Sparrow took over from Salim to take questions from the floor.

The BBC's boxing correspondent asked JJ why he thought he would win and posed the same question to Muller.

'For me it began on the streets of Salford. I had to know how to hurt somebody with my fists to protect myself, my family and my friends. You know boxing is like life, you can't win.' Watts smiled to himself. JJ was grossing ten million plus a streaming percentage. He was winning all the way to the bank.

Wolfgang Muller countered in the 'my life is tougher than yours' competition. 'I was sent to a Russian training school. A lot of my friends got psychologically broken or physically injured. I learned I was mentally tough as granite. You know I love to bleed, love it. People at ringside should bring umbrellas and plastic macs so they won't get splashed. Not my blood, but that jumped-up cruiserweight who thinks he can match my natural bulk, power and weight.'

Watts imagined Heather's dress polka dotted with blood in the front row.

JJ dropped the trash talk stone dead with a large dose of reality. He loved talking bollocks and would make a fortune on the after-dinner speaker circuit once he hung up his gloves. Not that he'd need the dough. 'Boxing is brutal. You might not come out of a fight the same way you went in.'

Watts agreed. Policing carried the same risks without the rewards, unless you were corrupt.

With the phoney war of words over, Samantha Sparrow thanked the boxers and said that was the end of the boxing Q&A. However, she said wanted to pay a tribute to John Budd, the police officer left brain-damaged preventing the abduction of Salim's wife, Zara. She said Salim and the main sponsor Baltic Power would have more to say on Saturday night, but Salim would like to say a few words direct to John, if he was watching. Salim spoke to the camera, said hello to his good friend, John Budd. 'Your brave spirit is with all of us and is a testimony to every one of us who puts others before themselves. My wonderful Zara is pregnant with our first born and if it is a boy we will call him Henna, John in Arabic, to honour our dearest friend.' Salim dipped his head slightly to show he'd finished, and Samantha took back the reins. 'During the incident 12 months ago, two of Zara's very special rings went missing. The police asked us not to mention it at the time for obvious reasons. We don't know what happened to them, but they are very precious family heirlooms to Salim and Zara. They have asked me to announce a £1m reward for the return of the rings with "no questions asked". We just want the rings back.'

Samantha ran through the telephone, email and social media contact details for anyone who wanted to discuss the rings, and showed close-up images of the jewellery on the screens behind her.

After the press conference was finished and the photo opportunities exhausted, Harry Quinn sidled over to Watts. 'Hello Nigel. Brought the rings with you? You've stopped coming down the QuinnGym?'

'Didn't feel right after John's injury.'

'Shannon's texted me. You chasing ghosts, Nigel?'

'That's my job.'

'Is it? I was reading human remains were found in a barrel in a receding reservoir near Las Vegas. Police reckon he was killed in the mid-seventies judging by his shoes. But who cares? The past belongs to yesterday, best ignored,' said Harry.

'And?' asked Watts.

'Let it go. Leave John Budd in his submerged barrel. Stop pestering my sister. She lost a son.'

'Shannon's not on my radar,' said Watts. 'I've never bet on a draw in boxing before.'

'Always a first time,' said Harry.

'Let's ditch the social niceties. Did you give John an advance nod about the result of the first fight, Harry?'

'Did he make a few quid?'

'You know the answer to that, I would imagine,' said Watts.

'Stop playing God, Nigel. Not a good look. Mind what you say, or you'll fall flat on your pompous face from your cloud in the sky.'

'About the draw?'

They smiled in grim silence, unable to decide how hard to push each other. Watts had the law on his side and Harry had muscle and money. Wasn't really a fair fight. The chief constable, Sir Richard Hurst, interrupted, oblivious of the stand-off. Harry excused himself, saying he couldn't leave JJ alone too long — the boxer was easily bored and distracted. Boxers were like small children. Let them out of your sight and they could start a riot. 'See you tomorrow, Nigel. You can watch from our corner, sit near us ringside. A special treat for an old friend.'

'You too, Harry. Wish JJ my best. Hope it's not another draw.'

'It won't be,' said Harry.

Harry winked and shook his head. Held up four fingers with a thumbs down. Watts said to himself JJ falls in the fourth round. That would be good odds. Was that Harry's unspoken thank you for protecting Shannon? John had bet thousands on the draw last time out and won handsomely. He hadn't needed to rob the Arabs but patience was not one of John's virtues. Watts could do the same, if Harry's nod and a wink was an accurate prediction. Would that count as corruption if he took financial advantage of a fixed fight? Why did Harry give John the nod? What favours had he done in return?

Alone, Hurst told Watts it was time to catch up informally. He had some really exciting, embargoed news that was strictly hush hush. 'I've been offered a once-in-a-lifetime opportunity that's impossible to resist. Salim had a proposition for me and I officially accept on Monday. I'm resigning as chief constable. I need good, honest people around me if you're interested. Give me time to settle in and for you to close down this John Budd business without attracting any embarrassing headlines first.'

Watts congratulated his old boss. The autocratic sports washers had purchased themselves a slick former chief constable to PR their involvement in western sporting activities. 'What do you mean?' asked Watts.

'Remember, Ed Boucher doesn't make or enforce the rules. We do. Or more specifically, you do. You're in charge of dealing with Ed Boucher and his nurse from now on. If you find enough evidence, arrest him, her or them.'

'Hie compensation request?'

'You decide. I've passed it over to you. Try not to compromise John's medal. It's the least the poor bastard deserves. Your colleagues won't appreciate you dropping him in the shit. Have you found any evidence to support or debunk these wild allegations?'

'No.' Watts zipped his lip. Hurst had stitched him up like a kipper. Cleverly removed himself from the firing line and left Watts to hoover up with integrity compromised.

Thirty-eight

Watts put a personal tab behind the bar at the Eagle and Child in Whitefield, a small gesture of thanks for the pro bono work carried out by the Code 66 detectives. If his plain-clothed colleagues working for free knew the truth about John, the mood would have been a lot less convivial. Watts reckoned they put the time in gratis because they imagined themselves in Budd's shoes. It could have been any one of them. How disappointing that the big man had let them down. 'Before we start, I knew nothing about the million-pound reward for the return of the rings. Complete shock to me and I don't know what they're trying to achieve. If anyone does find them, the next drinks are on them. Now let's exit fantasy world and get down to business. Tell me about the black VW Golf,' said Watts.

A detective stepped forward. He said the VW Golf belonged to bodybuilders, Jason and Jessica Long. They ran a gym in Whitefield and an online supplements store. He and another detective visited to ask about the car. They were very nervous having the police around, said they lent the vehicle to a house guest, a Ukrainian refugee named Angelina Kozar. She changed her name to Becky. Jessica thought she would find it easier getting work with an English name. Apparently, Angelina had had the car since 3rd May. They didn't know where the car was and hadn't spoken to Angelina. She had forgotten her passport and mobile and a bagful of clothes. A detective had them now.

They asked the couple why they weren't worried about lending a twenty grand car to someone they hardly knew? Jessica said Angelina had misunderstood Jason's hobby was filming him and his wife having sex. Angelina thought she was being asked to join in. A simple mistake friends make. All forgiven now. Jessica had helped Angelina to get an abortion, organised the delivery of a home termination kit.

Two other detectives stepped forward to say they had used automatic number plate recognition technology from the start of May. Tagged the search onto another investigation to satisfy privacy red tape. The first journey from Manchester to the Humber Bridge was early 4th May. The car travelled to Hull, York, Harrogate, Sunderland, South Shields, Durham, Wakefield, Leeds, Newcastle, Bradford and Huddersfield before docking back in Manchester. Now it was parked near the Malmaison hotel and hadn't moved for three days. The car's movements fitted with Nigel's honey-trapper narrative. Apart from a three-hour stop on the western side of the bridge. There were no hotels nearby and it was hardly a tourist attraction for homesick Ukrainians. They had done a bit of lateral thinking and had a theory. The bridge attracted suicides. Since the nineties, more than 200 people were reported to have jumped. Only five survived.

Another colleague looked into possible suicides. She had contacted the bridge staff and reviewed CCTV footage from 4th May. At five forty am they could clearly see two people in the middle of the bridge, fighting. A patrol officer intervened and escorted them eastwards to a car park. Dropped them off by an Audi with dealer plates. The patrolman said they were pissed and celebrating getting engaged. The detective called the holder of the dealer plate licence, who confirmed the person driving the car was Owen Chard. Owen had dropped the Audi in Hull and had never been back in touch. Cost the dealer a set of new plates.

One detective said a pragmatic suicide would drive onto the bridge, stop the car, get out, climb on the rails and jump. No procrastination. Or would have jumped in front of a train and avoided the bridge altogether. They all agreed the two wannabe suicides probably wanted to be stopped, him more than her.

'Tell me about dead Owen Chard?'

'You're talking to the wrong man, or woman' received a predictable laugh from officers who identified with the catchphrase of the TV tough-guy actor. The detective apologised for the bad taste impersonation. The poor bastard had kicked the bucket. His heart packed in after a night on the lash with Nigel's suspected honey-trappers. Looked fit as a butcher's dog on the bridge, even if he was in his fifties. Delivering cars was a big come down from red hot to couldn't catch a cold. TV and film producers might have frozen him out, but the tabloids got a lot of mileage from his drunken behaviour and unproven allegations of domestic violence made by his ex-wife before she emigrated to Canada with their kids.

Since 4th May, Owen had booked into hotels close to where the car had been parked. He used fictitious names, always paid in cash and always got a receipt. He always booked a double with the same second guest. She was young enough to be his daughter, but it looked to be purely a business relationship. There was no CCTV of them getting it on.

Roger, Owen's boss at the Edinburgh car dealers, said his friend was a bit of a Jack the Lad. Liked the booze and a toke through his nose. A bit of a womaniser if he got the chance, without being a sex-pest or a nuisance. Roger also said he had a couple of girlfriends. They were happy sharing him. He rented a room in a widow's house in Newhaven Avenue East in Edinburgh's city centre. She was on holiday, a cruise around the Norwegian fjords. They might have been fuck buddies. Roger's words, not the detective's.

The honey-trapping narrative was feasible. The Ukrainian was young, tall and pretty. Owen was handy with his fists. More time was needed to identify victims, although not anyone was going to admit to being snagged in a sex trap. Cash wise Owen lived by the skin of his teeth most of the time. A bit of a sad life. It might explain the bridge, said one of the detectives to a few nods of agreement.

'Tell me about Angelina Kozar.' A female detective took to the floor. As Nigel said, Angelina had extenuating circumstances. The detective handed a large envelope full of photographs and handwritten notes to Watts. Numerous

Russian war crimes websites listed the death of Angelina's husband Marko Kozar and his brother and cousin in Bucha. 'Could she have been tortured and raped?' asked Watts.

'Yes,' replied the detective.

Professionally, Angelina was a journalist, a health and social commentator. She had previously been a nurse. There were plenty of pieces online, but all in Ukrainian. She'd written a piece for the Guardian about declining birth rates in Ukraine. Year on year they were falling seven per cent. The drop was particularly noticeable after Russia's annexation of Crimea in 2014. Angelina had highlighted that Ukraine had one of the lowest birthrates on the planet before the war broke out. Who would want to bring up a child when they were exposed to Russian aggression?

'Family?'

Just her. Angelina. An orphan, brought up by her aunt. Mother Olga Kozar was killed in a car crash. She was well over the limit. Hit a tree and the tree won hands down.

'The father?'

No one named. The mum was in England when Angelina was conceived. Her name checked out on our database. Olga had made a very serious sexual assault allegation but the CPS said there was not enough evidence for a rape conviction. The alleged rapist was a famous footballer and TV celebrity who could afford the best barristers to make mincemeat of a state-funded overworked prosecutor and a young innocent Ukrainian woman out of her league.

'Do you have a name?' The female detective passed a piece of paper to Nigel. He looked at the name. Not enough evidence to obtain a conviction, according to the CPS. Did he even know he had conceived a child when he took Olga without her consent while she slept off a boozy lunchtime session in central Manchester? Sporting and TV celebrities were born lucky. Libel laws and their wealth protected them, helped by enablers who looked away if they earned off the celebrity.

'We're calling in lots of favours … and if that name gets released we're screwed at work and in the civil courts.'

'I know. Tell me about Ed Boucher?'

Two more detectives stepped forward. They said Ed lived in Hampshire and his parents were career diplomats. Prep school. Charterhouse. Read History at Oxford University. Joined the army as an officer. Graduated from Sandhurst. Toured Ireland, Afghanistan and Iraq. Got a commendation or two for bravery under fire. Saved a few lives when logistics chaps were injured by roadside bombs. Left the army in his late forties and joined the civil service. Worked in the Cabinet Office. A nominations assessor. A very boring ordinary middle-class man who did very ordinary boring things.

'Was he a drinker? A womaniser? A predator? A gambler? A racist? Anything they could use for leverage?' asked Watts.

Ed was none of the above. He played social cricket and tennis. Sailed and did a lot for charity on the south coast. Bit of a tragic personal life. Both parents dead in their fifties. Married Irene. She miscarried several times. They finally had a child, but Lucy, an unmarried mother, killed herself by jumping in front of the Bournemouth-Waterloo express. Her death was witnessed by her eleven-year-old child and her parents, who were standing next to her on the platform. Lucy was in her mid-twenties. Ed and Irene brought up Lucy's daughter, Alice, as their own. No mention of any father for orphan Alice, who joined the marines as an officer cadet. Completed basic training. Then quit. Off the record, she is alleged to have battered a couple of male cadets in a fight. Her training officer said she had massive potential, but didn't take to discipline or being told what to do. Since then, she had ploughed her energies into education. She was currently doing a masters in creative writing at a Manchester university.

'Is she in Manchester now?'

'It's term time, but she's missed a few sessions according to Martyn, her tutor.'

'Any pictures of her?'

'I'll zap them across. A pretty girl until she turned into a *Mad Max* extra.'

'What about the wife? Irene?'

Old money. The Lamb-Percy family goes back to the New Forest assassination of William Rufus. The fortune gets smaller generation after generation, but it is still substantial. Irene was in a care home with dementia, tragically struck down by the disease in her early fifties. She was in the home for her own protection. Boucher called every day until this week. The home thought he was on holiday or ill himself.

'Ordinary lives until you look deeper,' said Watts. He thanked them for their efforts. They had compressed so much research into one day and they didn't know how much they'd helped John Budd. 'There's a lot of hurt out there.' They applauded each other. They had busted a collective gut. No suspicious activity from Ed Boucher.

Watts had covered his tracks well. But they weren't looking for a blackmailer and never knew it was on the agenda. He apologised to his pro bono team. He had to go but there was plenty of cash behind the bar. They deserved a good night on the lash. If they were watching the boxing tomorrow, Heather and Hannah Budd would be in the ring before the big fight.

'No John?' asked one of the detectives.

'Sadly not. But miracles do happen if you have the money and the will.' Outside, Watts felt dirty, playing pig in the middle and conning everyone with his enforced disingenuousness. His colleagues deserved better. He deserved better. Why should he have to be judge, jury and executioner? He never signed up to play God. Never wanted to be compromised. Just wanted to capture and convict criminals. Now look at him. Potentially offering half a dozen of the bastards a free ride while he looked the other way. Frankie would leave him if she ever found out he was so pathetic.

Thirty-nine

Owen ordered a 35-day-aged rump steak, thin cut and cooked very rare so it was almost still alive. Alice selected half a corn-fed roasted chicken. They also ordered sautéed field mushrooms and broccoli. He had a bottle of BrewDog Punk IPA and she had a Coke. Said alcohol and her meds didn't mix. They were sitting in the Malmaison Bar & Grill fusion restaurant in the hotel, waiting on a call. There were two giants dwarfing the furniture sitting nearest the door. They looked gay. Owen supposed boxing fans weren't exclusively heterosexual. The German from the lift on the night Boucher died was there too with his woman. A lot less pissed than he had been in the foyer. Beyond the restaurant, he saw Angelina walk through the hotel doors. So different from when they had first bumped into each other on the Humber Bridge, the *CUTE BUT 101% PSYCHO* junkie a distant memory from the sensibly dressed woman sidestepping the drinkers at the bar. He was pleased to see her and blushed slightly. He hoped Alice didn't notice, that would be a sign of weakness. Ed's mobile was in the middle of the table and Owen willed the call to come through. 'Did you and Ed have a contingency for non-payment?

'They always paid because they believed the threat was real,' said Alice.

'And was it?' asked Owen.

'Yes. Was this the table Ed sat with Angelina the night he died?'

'You can ask Angelina now, if you like,' said Owen.

Owen introduced the two women. They said they'd already met. Waiting staff appeared and cleared a space. Angelina sat down and ordered an orange juice and a simple burger, nothing fancy on it. 'How do you know each other?'

'We met at Nina's. Alice is doing an MA in novel writing,' said Angelina.

'I am also Ed Boucher's granddaughter,' replied Alice.

'She knows about Ed's death,' said Owen, as if they were talking about the weather.

'I saw your video harassing him,' said Alice. 'Why is he tied to the bed?'

'To stop him raping me. He tried to fill me full of GHB. I'm sorry for your loss,' said Angelina.

'Owen said you tried to restart his cold heart,' said Alice.

'I failed,' said Angelina.

'If he'd survived, would you have told the police?' asked Alice.

'Yes. He needed to be stopped.'

'There was no evidence. No confession in your video,' said Alice. 'You were torturing him.'

'No offence,' said Angelina, 'but I don't care what you think. Forty countries sanction Russia. Two thirds of the world's population don't. They can all go and fuck themselves, like you can.'

'I'm on your side, Angelina. Ed only ever raped one person. Me. Me and Owen are going to write a song about him, aren't we? We just need a title,' said Alice.

'You want to celebrate and glorify rape?' asked Angelina.

'No,' said Alice. 'Never.'

'It's…it's…it's…' Angelina could not finish her sentence.

Alice reached across and stroked her hand. It was an act of tenderness Owen never imagined she possessed. 'I'm sorry. What happened to you. If I could …. I would,' said Alice.

'I know, everyone says that,' said Angelina. 'Did somebody called Samantha Sparrow ever contact you? She called your grandfather, said she had a letter for you.'

135

'We've both been busy,' said Alice.

From the corner of his eye, Owen noticed the drunken German headed towards them, hand outstretched. 'Hello. Couldn't help overhearing your conversation. My name is Hans Becker. My colleague is Ursula Bonn over there. We work for Baltic Power's international affairs department. We're Samantha Sparrow's colleagues. You just mentioned her?'

'Baltic Power?' asked Angelina. 'Is that a Russian-financed business?'

'We're talking to Ed and Alice, not you,' said Hans.

'What can we do for you?' asked Owen.

'You've not been in touch about our offer,' said Ursula, who had joined the group uninvited.

'You're not doing business with Baltic Power, are you?' Angelina asked Owen and then Alice. Held the stare with them both, daring them to say yes. Their silence was deafening.

'Our employer and the owner of Baltic Power, Viktor Andreyev, wants the names Samantha discussed with you, Edward. You remember your conversation at the train station?'

'Yes,' said Owen.

'You asked for a sparkling offer?'

'Yes.'

'He's ready to talk business, but is disappointed you've not contacted Samantha,' said Ursula.

'We're interested,' said Alice. 'We've evidence of a Lord plying fifteen-year-old boys with drinks before assaulting them. A current conservative MP who raped two women who wanted to work for him. A homeless charity boss who was sexually abusing fourteen-year-old boys in his care. Another Lord who had raped and assaulted children at a tennis club. And a TV celebrity linked to the far right who took indecent photographs of a four-year-old child alongside incitement to rape, murder, kidnap and torture.'

'Names? Proof?' asked Ursula.

'Money?' asked Alice. 'How much can Putin pay?'

'Nothing to do with him. Baltic wants intelligence about prospective partners within your Westminster bubble. Part of our international affairs remit. Influence governments to benefit our stakeholders,' said Hans.

'My joke about Putin. English humour. You Germans don't do nuance,' said Alice.

'We're not patient people either,' said Ursula.

'You're not going to send Mr Stretch to scare us?' grinned Alice. 'I've seen his powerful peashooter close up.'

Owen didn't have a clue what Alice was talking about, but he was happy she was winding Hans and Ursula up and not him.

'Viktor's only here for the fight. You and Ed can have a private chat at the Arena. Here are some tickets for you,' said Ursula. She placed two boxing tickets on the table. 'Come at least an hour before the main fight. Will only take five minutes.'

'Can I come?' asked Angelina. 'Viktor and I share a mutual heritage, according to profiles I've read online.'

'Why not? The more the merrier,' said Hans. Ursula handed over another ticket. Owen thought the chief constable was bound to be at the biggest sporting event in Manchester. He'd have to convince him that the John Budd exposure threat was real, like Alice had suggested.

FORTY

Watts knocked on the green door of Budd's double-fronted mid-terrace. It was late and he didn't want to spook the family and their carers by walking in unannounced. The box full of John's digital devices was still in his car. He'd get them later. Heather, in her pyjamas and a dressing gown, answered the door, a glass of wine in her right hand, mobile phone in her left. 'See you tomorrow,' said Heather, ending her call before pecking Watts on the cheek. 'That was Samantha Sparrow confirming what we were doing at the boxing. I'm nervous about it. Especially after the filming today. It's been a bloody nightmare. I feel violated. My house wasn't my own when the crew were here. A dozen people to film a video? We were all in one room and they were wandering around my house without any supervision. They could have been doing anything.'

'You know what media people are like,' said Watts, thinking the police would have been ten times worse.

'I saw the appeal from Salim on the TV. A million quid for the return of the rings. Is that true?'

'I know as much as you,' said Watts, noticing her breath stank of alcohol. He never visited this late normally so didn't know if it was a habit.

'They've never been in contact since the incident. No personal visits or phone calls to say thank you,' said Heather.

'They've donated lots of money to the trust fund,' replied Watts.

'Looks good for their PR.'

They went into the kitchen, where Heather ground fresh Blue Mountain beans, using a slow hand grinder. She boiled the kettle and poured the hot water over the beans in the black cafetière pot, then stirred and waited. Coffee late at night was not a great idea, but they were both stressed. Heather said Watts had just missed Helen Tapody. The neurosurgeon had talked about John's anticipated full recovery. There was a long road ahead, but she was an eternal optimist. 'Helen is delusional. Wants to win the most "compassionate Aussie of the year" award, if that's not a contradiction in terms,' said Heather. 'John's fucked.'

'Talking about carers, recognise her?' asked Watts. He was surprised by the venom in Heather's voice. He held up a picture. Heather inspected the image and put her glasses on to take a closer look.

'We've had so many carers. Been like Piccadilly station at rush hour. I'll ask Hannah. The young ones like her better than me,' said Heather. 'I'm just a bitter old crone with vinegar tits.'

'And your bad points?'

They laughed half-heartedly. Heather went into John's room and came out a minute later. 'Alice Lamb-Percy. Worked for a couple of months towards the end of the last year,' said Heather. 'She was on a creative writing course.'

'Do they keep handwritten notes about visits?' asked Watts.

She led Watts into the sitting room and looked under the television for the care logs that detailed visits. She handed them to Watts, who searched for notes written by Alice Lamb-Percy. He took several photographs. Would her writing match the abuse letter? Changing the subject, Watts told Heather the devices were in his car and did she want them back? 'No rush. He's not going to need them anytime soon. Did you find anything of interest?' Heather asked.

'John had two online gambling accounts,' said Watts. 'Do you know about them?'

'No,' said Heather. 'How much does he owe?'

'We couldn't access them,' lied Watts.

'Nobody's chased any debts,' said Heather. 'He must be in credit. I was terrified of being skint when he was hurt. If he died, there wouldn't be compensation enough to last mine and Hannah's lifetimes. That's why I kept them.'

'Kept what?'

'Don't be cross with me.'

'I won't. Kept what?'

'I found them in John's belongings when I collected his clothes in A&E. Recognised everything apart from the two rings,' said Heather.

'How come you never told me?' asked Watts.

'Was scared that you might think he'd stolen them.'

'Why would anyone think that? John never had a chance to hand them over to the police so he could hardly be accused of pinching them,' said Watts.

'I wasn't thinking straight. There was no mention of the rings until today. You never mentioned it. Sir Richard didn't. Why should I connect them?'

'You have done now,' said Watts. 'What's changed?'

'That £1m reward.'

'Where are they?' Heather untied the cord around the waist of her dressing gown and undid all the buttons of her green and white striped pyjama top. A gold necklace with two rings was hanging between her exposed cleavage. 'Have they been there all the time?' asked Watts, focusing on the rings and avoiding the floppy dog's ears.

'Where better? My body is a no-go zone,' said Heather. 'Forget the rings. You know, I never understood why John let the taxi hit him full on. It was almost like he wanted it to mow him down. Like he had a premonition about his future and knew suicide was the only option for him.'

'Forget about John for a minute, I'm more concerned about the rings,' said Watts. 'Why did you not tell anyone for twelve bloody long months?'

'I don't know. You're the one with the detection skills,' said Heather.

'I don't know the answer either, Heather,' said Watts. 'That's why I'm asking you.'

'Fuck all this shit. I wish I'd copped off with you that fateful night in the Cyprus Tavern. My life would be a lot less complicated with a good, honest man like you, Nigel,' said Heather. She played with the rings on the end of the gold chain. 'The bloody rings are cursed. Like the genie in the lamp. Rub them and evil spirits are released.'

'And what would you wish for, if you freed the ring genie?' asked Watts.

'I wish John would die. Right now. This minute. Kick the bucket. Imagine the relief for us all,' said Heather. 'Will they give me a million quid, no questions asked, like they said on the TV?'

'It is a PR stunt. It's not a real offer,' said Watts.

'I wish you could hold me tight, Nigel, like when a man loves a woman. Take me away from this bloody mess.'

Watts poured the coffee and added milk. Took two sugars for extra energy. He was tired. Drained through lack of sleep and stress. His best friend's wife wanted her husband dead. In mitigation, she was exhausted after twelve months of unimaginable suffering. 'Neither of us would want to disappoint Frankie or ourselves,' said Watts. He reached across. Held the chain around Heather's neck. Pulled it and her closer to him. Their lips and eyes were inches apart. If they poked out their tongues they would touch. She was breathing heavily. Her top gaped, tiny goosebumps over her chest. He inspected the jewellery. Both rings had blood on them. Knife marks where a blade had chopped at the finger. 'You're playing with dynamite Heather. Those rings will get you hurt.'

Heather pulled her head away from his and removed his fingers from the rings. She pushed his hand away and sat back, straightening her shoulders and puffing out her chest. She oozed belligerence. He was seeing a different harder, harsher side to her. Had she always been like that, and he never noticed because they were friends? 'What're you going to do Nigel?

'You going to confess?'

'I've not done anything wrong. Nor has John. Nor has Hannah, your goddaughter. You swore on a bible to take responsibility for the Hannah's spiritual development and stand as an example of a person with faith in God,' said Heather. 'Do your duty.'

'And yours?'

'Stop being a pompous arse, Nigel. No room for sentimental fools.'

'Do up your top. Give me the rings — or keep them and face the consequences.' Watts looked at her and knew he was caught in a trap. There was a narrative evolving that disgusted Watts. One way or another, he was going to make a right tit of himself. A Mancunian Lee Harvey Oswald, the alleged lone wolf assassin of John F Kennedy, the single most horrific global tragedy of the second half of the last century. A patsy to carry the can for the establishment's corruption and cynicism. 'You two deserve each other.'

'John's still your best friend. You're like brothers. Do right by him, me and Hannah,' said Heather, carefully doing up her top's buttons.

SATURDAY 11TH JUNE 2022
FORTY-ONE

Owen watched the 24-hour news on mute. Subtitles told the story behind the depressing looped images and video clips. The £1m Budd rings reward had gone viral. Drone footage showed Mancunian fortune-hunters had descended on the Pomona Strand wasteland in Salford Quays. Groups of divers in full scuba gear were dropping into the River Irwell and the Bridgewater Canal. There was even a report that an ambulance, believed to have taken John Budd to the hospital almost a year ago, was stopped overnight and searched for half an hour by a gang of youths armed with knives, bottles and Molotov cocktails.

Owen was a worried man. The chief constable was as silent as the hotel TV. Owen didn't have a mobile number to call, he would have to wait until the boxing tonight on the off chance of bumping into the top cop who literally held his future prosperity in his hands. He was waiting on a phone call that wasn't going to be made. The chief had called his bluff, and Owen was powerless to put on any pressure on him. Was it time to run before they kicked down the door? He had cash and a false ID that was meant to be used by dead Ed Boucher. He could use it if he kept Alice sweet and she gave him a free ride.

Angelina's gentle snoring interrupted his thoughts. Why did he think she was a drug addict and not pregnant on the bridge? His mind was a sewer. His ex-wife had been sick in the morning loads when she had the girls. He'd sung *Honky Tonk Woman* to himself every time she chucked. He'd just been asked to direct *The Termination*, a bloody 48-hour off-Broadway production starring a pregnant Angelina Kozar and a fistful of pills. He'd read the abortion script several times last night. Angelina's kit contained five abortion pills. One Mifepristone. Four Misoprostol. Ibuprofen to numb the physical pain, Flagyl to combat internal infection, sanitary towels to mop up blood during the first 24-hours of cramps, diarrhoea, vomiting and excessive bleeding. Angelina said she would kick off the process this morning, take the Mifepristone to ready her body to eject the foetus. She would wait 24 hours until Sunday am. Insert the Misoprostol deep inside her vagina. Let 'nature' finish off the bloody deed. There was a major script development problem from Owen's perspective. The dates didn't add up. Last night she'd given him a Bucha timeline. Safe sex with her husband. Unprotected sex with a rapist Russian soldier. She'd been emphatic about the abortion. My body, my mind, my choice. Owen checked the dates online and used a pregnancy calculator. Angelina was around 14 weeks — that meant they needed a doctor. Without one, there was a one in ten chance she would need help to remove foetus debris from inside a womb. She might suffer permanent damage and it could threaten her ability to have children in the future. In extreme circumstances, her life was at risk.

Were they finally going to be honest with each other? More to the point, was he going to be honest with himself? Stop using being an actor as an excuse for poor behaviour and bad decisions?

She opened her blue-green eyes and focused on him. It took her a second or two to adjust to her surroundings and she looked terrified, then it clicked. Owen could see her relax when she recognised a familiar safe face. He'd forgotten how good that felt. To be wanted. Needed. 'Shall we start?' asked Angelina.

'Is it really safe?'

'Thousands of women are having abortions across Europe, across the world. Irrespective of my own personal circumstances, giving birth during a war is not fair on anyone. Me, the child, or those who have to look after us.

I cannot do it by myself. I am fragile, not wood,' said Angelina.

'Fourteen weeks pregnant. Your last period the middle of March. The assault and conception at the end of March. An ultrasound confirms you're pregnant on a Tuesday ...,' said Owen.

'And a failed suicide on the Wednesday,' said Angelina. 'Let's pretend I didn't know the dates.'

'We know that would be a lie.'

'What's one more untruth?' asked Angelina. 'Only me and you will ever know. Same as our honey-trapping and identity theft.'

'There's an alternative. That piece of paper Nina Mazur gave you with the details of the clinic. I've checked online. We could book a same-day abortion in South Manchester,' said Owen.

'I don't want to be on the record,' said Angelina.

'We can pay cash. I'll pay. No one will ever check the records.'

'Promise?'

'Promise. Bucha wasn't your fault. Putin was responsible. Andrei Orlov's rape wasn't down to you.'

'He's still the father, even with half his head missing,' said Angelina.

'Forget him. You could still be a mother,' said Owen. 'Your friends and family will rally around. In Manchester or the Ukraine.'

'And the child? What if it grows up and wants to kill because murder is in its genes? What happens when it wants to know about its "Dad" and asks were we in "love"? What do I say then? I was prepared to kill myself to stop my unwanted child being born. Daddy was a war criminal rapist who died in a ditch.'

'Wars are different,' said Owen.

'Are they? This war could last two, three, four years. A decade. A generation. As long as other countries support Putin, he can fight forever. And they will. Already the will to oppose him is weakening. If Trump wins the next election, the war is fucked. Only Putin's death offers a peaceful end. Or does it? His successor could be worse.'

A knock on the door interrupted their discussions. For a split micro-second, Owen pictured the chief constable with a sack full of uncut diamonds slung over his shoulder. He opened the door. No riches. Just Detective

Inspector Watts carrying a black plastic bin. He looked like he was going to church or taking unwanted clothes down to the local charity shop. Owen knew he was either going to get paid or arrested.

FORTY-TWO

Alice left Stretch cracking zeds in his bed and let the door close silently behind her. She tiptoed down the corridor of the top floor of the Dakota hotel and stopped for a second. Alice had been waiting half her life for this moment. She used Stretch's security pass to enter Samantha's room. The PR consultant was fast asleep in her double bed, wearing ears muffs and an eye mask. Alice turned on the lights, sat on the bed and lifted the muffs and mask. She cupped her hand over Samantha's mouth. With her other hand, she gently shook Samantha's shoulder until she stirred and instantly stiffened with fear. 'Sorry to disturb you like this. It's Alice. Alice Lamb-Percy.' Samantha, initially wide-eyed and terrified, relaxed.

'Bloody hell, Alice, can't you arrange normal meetings like everyone else? What the fuck do you want?'

'I believe your father — my father — left me a letter?'

'You need to sign for it, according to his solicitor,' said Samantha.

'Let's go for it,' said Alice. She stepped back to let Samantha climb out of bed.

'You're weird, Alice,' said Samantha. The PR opened her briefcase. Produced an envelope. She took out another envelope and a piece of paper that she unfolded, and passed it and a pen to Alice who signed. 'Here you are.'

Alice took the letter, sat on the bed and opened it. She pulled out expensive writing paper with an embossed address, then looked inside the envelope to see if anything else was enclosed. There was a lock of blonde hair and a tiny baby tooth. Little bits of her as an innocent child? Alice read the handwritten letter two or three times and passed it to Samantha.

'Here. No secrets between half-sisters.'

3.4.22

Dear Alice

If you're reading this letter, the odds are pretty high that I am dead. I've just had a visit from your grandfather, who has accused me of under-age sex. This is my confession to you. My guilt. My crime. I had a very loving relationship with your mother, Lucy, that started when she was fifteen and a schoolfriend of my own Samantha. Our age difference didn't make our love any less relevant or intense. And if I had been a stronger, better man, I would have chosen Lucy over my wife and damned the torpedoes when you were born. Sorry. Writing this is so hard. I am being as honest as I can. Life isn't simple and I had too much to lose if I acknowledged you as my daughter and took financial and emotional responsibility for you. My loss. When you were born, me and your mother stayed away from each other. Lucy and my child were so close and yet so far. Villages apart. Country lanes apart. Although she did send me a lock of your hair a week after you were born. And the first baby tooth that fell out of your mouth. And a picture of your christening. Then she stopped communicating completely and I let her go. When she fell from that train platform, I was heartbroken. The coroner said it was an open verdict, but I knew. It was because of our unrequited love. My life was never the same again and acknowledging you would hurt too much. I was wrong. I treated her and you badly and unkindly. You know, we picked your name between us. Alice because she — and you — lived in wonderland. Why am I telling you this now when I am gone? I suppose everyone needs to know where they come from and how they got here. I am sorry you've not grown up with Samantha, Clive, Jeremy and Alex. They are good kids. Loving, loyal children. I will leave it to your discretion should you wish to share this letter with them.

Best wishes

Rupert (Dad)

PS: now you've received this letter, please contact my lawyer Dill Forni. He will give you access to a trust fund in your name. Use it to pay for university or a deposit on a house or travelling around the world.

Samantha read the letter and sat down on the bed beside Alice, crying gently. 'Bloody Lucy. Long legs and big tits. Was my dad really having sex with a schoolgirl my age? She must have seduced my father at the tennis club. Disgusting. Jesus Christ, this is so fucked up.'

'Didn't you ever know about your "secret" half-sister?' asked Alice.

'No,' replied Samantha. She wiped the tears away with the back of her hand. 'Of course not. But I wish I did. I have three brothers. I was always the tomboy with grazed knees and elbows. I always wanted a sister to play house and push prams and dress up.'

'Now you've got one,' said Alice.

'Did my father kill himself because of Ed? I'll have him arrested before my brothers kill him.'

'Too late. My grandfather died the night you saw him at the station. There's been a mix-up with the identification of the body. I'm going to the undertakers to check in person. Do you want to come?' asked Alice.

'I'm too busy with work to deal with this now. Once tonight is over we can talk more,' said Samantha. 'Book an appointment with my office next week. How did you find out my dad was your dad?'

'DNA.'

'Why him?'

'I saw my mum and Ed in bed and thought he was my Daddy. She told me it was somebody else very much like grandpa, but nicer, kinder.'

'Did she mention him by name?' asked Samantha.

'No. I checked out all the potential dads who loved young teens in Hampshire,' said Alice. 'Compiled a list.'

'What a fucked-up world you live in. Were you in on the blackmail too?' asked Samantha. 'Is it your sex-pest list all along. Did you force my dad to kill himself?'

'No. I wanted him to come clean and publicly acknowledge me,' said Alice.

'How did you get his DNA?'

'He thought he was mentoring Kitty Elms, a first year sixth former studying media,' said Alice. 'I took a sample of his DNA at his flat.'

'Jesus Christ, that's the name in his diary the week he died. You're as devious as your grandfather. I'm not sure to congratulate you or smack you,' said Samantha.

'Good luck with that,' smiled Alice. The first thing the Royal Marines had taught her was how to kill people with her bare hands. She put those skills into practice when two dumb Marines noticed her scars and misread mental health challenges as a spit-roast invite.

'That's either genius or a stalker nightmare. All too much for me to digest. You'd better go and identify Ed. We still want your grandfather's sex-pest list. Redact Rupert, for obvious reasons. Tonight would be a good time to hand it over in person to Viktor. Did you fuck my dad?'

'We tried,' said Alice. 'He was a gas shag, struggled to get it up. I think I was too old.'

The disgust on Samantha's face said it all. The look of pure revulsion said they had no future as sisters. Be careful what you wish for because your expectations will never be realised. Alice had expected so much more from the grand reveal, yet Samantha's hypocrisy working for Baltic and wanting sex-pest dirt was just as seedy as her own behaviour. At least Alice knew she was a shit person. If Samantha had behaved like a true sister, Alice would have told her about Stretch's involvement in Rupert's demise. Despite the disappointment, on the plus side Alice didn't want to cut herself.

FORTY-THREE

Owen guessed his luck had run out when he answered the door. An expressionless Watts was outside the hotel room. Time to face the music. Owen stepped aside and gave the detective space to walk in the room and expected others to follow him, except he was flying solo and had made no attempt to arrest him. 'Do we need lawyers or a wealth advisor?'

'You're a very funny man, Owen, and a pretty convincing actor,' replied Watts. 'Mind if I have a look around?'

'Be my guest,' said Owen, undecided what was the nature of Watts' game. If he wasn't arresting him, maybe he wanted his cut. Everyone had a price.

Watts casually walked around the room, picking up Ed's things that were scattered around the room, Ed's mobile, Ed's wallet, Ed's briefcase, Ed's old school tie and red braces, Ed's John Budd folder and Ed's heart and blood pressure pill case. He inspected them closely and took his time and then put them down again, slowly.

Watts looked in the wardrobe at two of Boucher's jackets and trousers neatly hung up, the expensive shirt, the scuffed Dr Marten shoes were in stark contrast to the rest of the expensive clobber. He picked up the kill pills, the Mifepristone, Misoprostol, Ibuprofen and Flagyl and the packs of sanitary towels. Put them down again too and closed the door, slowly.

'What's going on?' asked Angelina, waking and rising from the bed.

'I could ask you two the same thing,' said Watts. 'I've come to have a private word with Owen. Could you give us ten minutes? Go for a coffee downstairs.'

'Owen's dead. This is Ed,' said Angelina. She quickly pulled on a top and jeans from a chair beside the bed.

'Sorry, I want a private word with Ed. Go grab a coffee, Ed's friend.'

'Who are you?'

'A police detective. DI Nigel Watts. Are you his co-conspirator?'

'She's innocent. Aren't you going to South Manchester? Visiting that antique shop we talked about?' said Owen.

'Not without you.'

'Wait downstairs, Ed's friend.'

'My name is Angelina.'

'I know who you are. Don't go far,' said Watts. 'This bag belongs to you. Smells musky. Jason and Jessica never washed your clothes. Your Ukrainian passport in on top. I'm sorry about what happened to you in Ukraine. I can ask specialist trauma colleagues to chat with you. I can call my wife. She's a psychoanalyst and won't judge. Everything's off the record.'

Angelina looked blankly at Watts as if she didn't understand what he was saying. She turned to Owen for his approval to leave him alone with the detective. Owen nodded and she left without saying thank you.

'Your wife is a good-looking woman. Where did you meet?' Before Owen could improvise a suitable reply, Watts answered his own question. 'Does the Humber Bridge on 4th May ring a bell? Not long enough for you to get her pregnant.'

'You're talking to the wrong man.'

'That's funny, Owen. I see what you did there. Using Billy Whyte's catchphrase. You should do stand-up when you get out of prison.'

'How much do you want?' asked Owen.

'Will she wait for you? Your fake wife? Even after you smack her about? Or is that all part of your method acting skills? If you've murdered Ed Boucher, that's life. Blackmail and fraud are pretty serious crimes in their own right. You'll be seventy-five or eighty before you get out.' Watts held his hands up to stop Owen from interrupting him. 'You can't deny the DNA. How did Ed die? Don't answer. An autopsy will tell us. Or do you want to give me your version, your truth?' asked Watts. 'Explain why you're pretending to be Ed Boucher, having faked your own death?'

'On or off the record? As I said, I think you're talking to the wrong man. Chat to Sir Richard Hurst.'

'Are you hoping the jury will sympathise with you, because you and Angelina aren't criminals at heart? She's been brutalised by the Ukraine war. You're famous enough to get off too. Mr Happy-Go-Lucky with your good looks and sense of humour. A jury will decide you're dumb opportunists. Stumbled on a scam. The real criminals are the late Ed Boucher and his granddaughter, Alice Lamb-Percy. You can blame her as the mastermind behind your failed blackmail plot. Help us convict her after you and Angelina resolve the dead body mix up without any police involvement. With a bit of luck and a fair wind, you both fly away from Manchester free as birds,' said Watts, determined somebody should be held to account.

'Pay me fifty grand and I'll give you Alice for free,' said Owen, thinking that would be poetic justice for her fucking him without his consent and scaring the shit out of him. 'The money will give me a year to sort my life out.'

Before Watts could answer, his mobile rang. The phone was loud enough for Owen to hear a male voice say that a woman was wanting to see Owen Chard's body. She said she was a relative and what should the caller do? Watts said stall her for forty-five minutes and that he was coming over. 'A stalemate won't help anyone.' Watts took out a ticket for the boxing and handed it to Owen. 'I'll see you there about eight. Go to your seat for the undercard fights as Owen Chard. I'll have your money.'

Owen tried to keep a straight face. Fifty wasn't a quarter of a million but it was still better than a kick in the nuts. He already had ten grand he'd pinched from Ed, and he wouldn't be sharing his winnings with Angelina. She didn't know about his bonanza and it was him taking all the risks, so he deserved all the profits.

Forty-four

Watts guessed it would be Alice Lamb-Percy. He was proved right when he walked into the undertakers. Old Tosh greeted him, showed him through to the waiting area where Alice was sitting in an expensive dress and a cashmere jumper. Butter wouldn't melt, until you noticed the piercings and the tattoos. She looked very young and welcomed him with a broad smile. Old Tosh introduced him as Nigel, a friendly off-duty police officer. They shook hands. 'I believe you're here to see Owen Chard's body. Are you related?' asked Watts.

'No,' replied Alice.

'Tosh asked me to have a word with you. We can't let just anyone see a body. They need to be next of kin or close family. Can I see some ID first to prove you're who you say you are?' asked Watts. 'What's your relationship to Owen Chard?'

Alice handed Watts her passport and driver's licence. Old Tosh said he would need a form signed before he prepared the body for viewing. Health and safety regulations meant they had to be very careful not to damage the body in transit. 'You've got the wrong dead man,' said Alice. 'I think you've got my granddad in the fridge. Edward Boucher, not Owen Chard.'

'Why do you say that?' asked Watts.

'Owen Chard is very much alive,' said Alice. She burst into tears. Old Tosh stepped forward automatically, a box of tissues in his hand. She grabbed a handful, noisily blew her snotty nose, wiped her eyes and regained her composure. 'Me and him are fuck buddies.'

Watts apologised on behalf of the police and said he worked serious crimes, murder and organised crime. Blackmailing and fraud and false representation rarely fell under the serious crimes banner, unless there were exceptional circumstances. He explained she would need to make a statement to uniformed officers about the identity mix-up. Administrative errors were not his domain, it was a coincidence he was here at all. Watts and his wife Frankie were shopping and then he was off to see the big fight tonight. He was giving Tosh a spare ticket as his mate couldn't make it. Alice nodded, completed the form and handed it back to Old Tosh. He left it on the table and Watts checked the writing. Not the same as the fake allegation letter or the log entries in John Budd's care book. She was clever, her blackmail scam was pretty sophisticated but the experts would suss out any similarities. She might be smarter than Chard and Kozar, but all criminals made mistakes. Everyone did, although the consequences were different.

Inside the undertaker's viewing room, Ed Boucher was laid out on a gurney covered in a blanket. Old Tosh lifted the cover to reveal Ed's head. Alice spat at the dead man. Her spittle landed on the bridge of his nose, ran down his cheek. 'The bastard. It's him. May his soul rot in hell. If you knew what he'd done to me.'

'Do you want to tell me about it?'

'Privately. He needs to go.' She nodded at Tosh.

'Give us a bit of time,' said Watts.

'Shall I put him away first?' asked Tosh.

'Do you want to go outside or find a more comfortable room?' Watts asked Alice.

'It's fine here. What's your name?'

'Detective Inspector Nigel Watts,' he replied.

'Why should I trust you?' asked Alice.

'My job is to protect ALL citizens, and that includes you.'

'You look friendly enough.'

'Thank you for the reference,' said Watts. 'I can help you, that's for sure. But you don't have to talk to me about personal stuff. We have specialist officers who are trained to talk to victims or survivors. Give you the support that is beyond me. I can drive you to them now, or they can come to you. Entirely up to you? If you prefer a female to help you, it will take a few minutes to organise.'

'I'll tell you why I spat at him. I tried to manage him. I spent my teens making sure he only hurt me. I'm twenty-one years of age and feel ninety after his abuse. For ten years the only way to control him was to sleep with him. Let him act out his sexual fantasies on me.'

'I'm very sorry to hear that,' said Watts.

'Ed used to abuse his wife, Irene. Beat her, my grandmother. Choked her until she was unconscious. Chipped away at her self-confidence until she was too anxious to think for herself. Dementia was a blessing. A release from the torture that he inflicted on her every single day of her sad life,' said Alice.

'Do you know how he died?' asked Watts. 'How come you suspected he was here?'

'Somebody stole his identity. Claimed an actor died when he's still very much alive. Here, look at this.' Alice showed Watts a video. Owen on the bed, on her mobile.

'Is that Owen Chard and you having sex?'

'Sex or rape. How do you define consent?' asked Alice. 'I like it rough, but I do like to be asked in advance. I have to hurt to feel. What about you?'

'Do you want to make a complaint against Owen Chard?' asked Watts. 'I'm off-duty, but I can ask my female colleagues to come out now. Discuss Owen and your late grandfather. They can look after you. Get you the help you need.'

'It's not me who needs the help,' said Alice. 'I'm too far gone for help.'

'What do you mean?'

'Ed blackmailed people. A certain kind of people. People who liked children. People with money who would pay Ed for his silence. Bribed him to look the other way.'

'How do you know this?'

'I was his accomplice, his researcher. I found the victims online. In

156

survivor chat groups. Befriended them. Identified them and their abusers. I could have been a detective like you. Once he was briefed, Ed confronted famous establishment figures. We were paid a "crisis management" fee to make their problem disappear.'

'Be careful, you could be incriminating yourself,' said Watts, unsure why he was cautioning her to careful about what she said when she was going down for her crimes.

'None of the abusers will admit to being blackmailed by Ed. The survivors want to be left alone. I'm telling you because I'm free now Ed's gone. I want to have a clean conscience. Mandy needs help.'

'Who's Mandy?'

'The woman John Budd abused. I know about Owen meeting you and Sir Richard.'

'Is her blackmail letter real?'

'Yes.'

'Who is she?'

'She wants to stay anonymous.'

'Without her making a statement, there is no case to answer,' said Watts. 'The letter isn't enough. It can't be authenticated and could be a fiction. Any defendant, including John Budd, would walk free.'

'John Budd will never walk anywhere,' said Alice. 'He's as incapacitated as my mother was when I pushed her in front of a train.'

'You're unloading an awful lot on me, Alice. Are you playing silly buggers?'

'No,' she said, and she told him about the death of her mother Lucy at Winchester station when she was a small child.

When she had finished, she asked Watts what happened next. Was he going to arrest her for confessing to the murder of her own mother on the railway platform and all the other crimes she has committed? Before Watts could answer, she pulled out a knife, flicked it open and held it to her throat. A millimetre away from ending her life.

FORTY-FIVE

A male officer interviewed Owen. The actor had dropped the Ed impersonation and come to the party as himself. A female constable interviewed Angelina, kitted out in a loose flowing floral dress in anticipation of what was to follow their confessions. The duo was interrogated in two interview rooms side by side in a city centre police station. Owen and Alice had promised to stick to the truth and play their respective suicide cards.

Owen piled on the charm. Explained how he struggled to come to terms with his dwindling acting career. Forced himself to deliver secondhand cars to make ends meet once he had stopped being Billy Whyte three times a week.

His interviewer sympathised. Said he liked his portrayal of the renegade police officer up to his neck in filth.

Owen thanked him and said he wished casting directors felt the same way towards him. Whenever he got a script nowadays, he'd only read the first act because whatever character he was going to play would meet a gruesome, violent death within the first thirty minutes. That got a good laugh from the interviewer. He talked about being on the Humber Bridge early one morning in the Spring. Everyone thought he was a strong man, but most of the time he was pretending, acting. He said he'd talked himself out of suicide and decided to do some living before he died. Like alcoholic depressive Ben, played by Nicolas Cage in *Leaving Las Vegas*, who drank himself to death in the company of a sex worker, Sera, played by Elisabeth Shue. Owen could see the interviewer was transfixed with the power of the story about the movie although he was too young to have seen the film when it came out in 1995, or to have read the book by John O'Brien. The author, like the lead in the movie, killed himself — but with a gun rather than booze. Owen said he had met Ed Boucher in a city centre boozer. They decided to swap identities as a joke. See who could chat up women best. Ed, masquerading as the cracked actor, copped off with a Ukrainian refugee. Owen, depressed again, said he'd gone to a bothy in the Scottish Highlands for some space. Imagine his surprise when he got back to Manchester and found he had died. People were mourning his passing. He went to the Malmaison where Boucher was staying, found Angelina and hey presto, he was clearing the air. 'Are we good to go?' asked Owen.

'After you've signed your witness statement,' said the officer. 'If we need any more information we'll be in touch. I'll check out the *Leaving Las Vegas* movie. A true story?'

'As much as they can be,' said Owen.

An hour later, a tired Angelina emerged from the interview room with two female officers. One in uniform, one in plain clothes.

Outside, Owen asked Angelina how come she had taken so long. She replied that if they wanted it to be authentic, she had to go into detail about Boucher's attempted rape. 'You told them the truth?' asked Owen.

'Yes. We're clearing up our mistakes,' said Angelina. 'Now we need to focus on getting rid of the unwanted invader. Where is Alice?'

Probably in police custody, thought Owen. If Watts was any good at his job, he'd have nicked her and then sectioned her. She was a one hundred percent nut job who was no longer in his orbit.

FORTY-SIX

Watts stayed iceberg cool. Don't overreact and lose control. Was Alice going to cut her throat? The knife was close to her neck. She gripped the handle like she knew how to use it. She had alleged her dead blackmailing grandfather abused her over a sustained period. She had conspired with him to blackmail abusers, including John Budd. She may or may not be accusing Owen Chard of rape. Alice even suggested she might have killed her mother at a train station in Winchester, aged eleven years. Alice could have been a detective like Watts, except it's not a hobby. You have to serve a twenty-year apprenticeship to learn the skills to contextualise crime. But he'd never done any hostage-taking courses. 'I'm so sorry what's happened to you. I'm not surprised you're upset and feeling hurt. We can work through this together,' said Watts.

'Detective to detective?' asked Alice.

'Horrendous being on the station platform when your mother was killed. You must be feeling very hurt after all that's happened to you,' said Watts, aware if she cut her throat the John Budd blackmail scam died with her. If he paid Chard his fifty grand from Budd's gambling winnings, the elephant in the room would be free. No crimes had ever been committed. Nobody could be charged and convicted.

'Possibly,' she replied.

The knife was still poised at her jugular and her eyes were focused on Watts. He daren't look away in case he appeared to be disinterested. She was as abused as Angelina Kozar and deserved to be treated with the same compassion and care. You couldn't differentiate between victims. They were all equal in their suffering. He couldn't let Angelina go and still try and punish Alice. 'There are a whole load of things I don't understand.'

'Like?'

'Is an eleven-year-old girl physically strong enough to push an adult in front of a train? Even if the adult is caught unawares?'

'Possibly,' said Alice.

'She'd have to be standing right on the edge of the platform to fall onto the tracks just as the train arrived.'

'My grandparents never spoke about it. Banned me, too. I had no recollection of pushing her. But I didn't have any memory of not pushing her. What should I believe?' asked Alice.

'My wife Frankie says personal memories are closer to fiction than fact.'

'Is she a writer?'

'A psychoanalyst.'

'Sounds very posh.'

'She's fascinated by false memories and whether therapists implant memories of childhood sexual abuse.'

'Or whether women sometimes misremember consensual sex as rape?' asked Alice. 'And do you believe her?'

'We're still married. She says our minds aren't computers. Memories don't exist. Each time we recall something, we engage in a creative reconstruction. She says they change constantly because we do. We edit our pasts to ensure the future is written with us shown in the best possible light.'

Alice nodded. 'What do you think of that, Ed? This detective is implying memories are self-serving. I might be suffering from reverse false memory syndrome. Did you plant bad thoughts in my head? Did you do the same with Lucy?'

For a second, Watts thought Alice was about to mutilate the corpse.

According to Frankie, there was a fallibility about historic eyewitness testimony, based on recovered memories. Frankie said memories of traumatic events were buried. People were motivated to forget. Seeing her grandfather dead had resurrected horrible experiences. Frankie called it dissociative amnesia.

Alice handed the knife to Watts.

He took it.

He nodded at her and then at Old Tosh from behind a window in the corridor. The attendant entered the room and wheeled dead Ed back to the cooler. 'That man lying there is Edward Boucher, my grandfather. All I've just said is made up bollocks. The abuse. The raping. The blackmail. The train station malarky. I've got a syndrome. Maybe two or three. I act weird when I'm stressed. The police don't have the resources for a mental health crisis. We're on our own. Catching water in a net. Whatever you should do, you won't. You want John Budd to get his George Cross more than you want to help the likes of me, Mandy and Angelina. Do I need to sign anything identifying Ed?'

Alice was right. There was a police crib sheet with boxes to tick. He could refer her to the overstretched mental health services. They would book her an appointment three months down the road. He could arrest her and tie up half a dozen officers for months. Eventually, she would be charged with running around Manchester with a big mouth and John and Heather Budd would both be disgraced. Hannah would have nobody. 'Do you want a lift anywhere after you've signed the paperwork?'

'That's very kind. An abortion clinic in South Manchester,' said Alice.

'It's on my way,' lied Watts. While they were driving across the city centre, Alice dropped her final bombshell. 'There's one thing I do want to officially report. It is about the murder of Rupert Sparrow. His killers are in Manchester. They're with Baltic Power and are flying out this weekend, possibly even as early as tonight. I've got video evidence of them leaving Sparrow's flat after they threw him out of the window. Give me your number and I'll ping you the file,' said Alice. 'Once I've given you my statement, I'll need anonymity, maybe even witness protection. Those bastard friends of Putin and Baltic Power owner Viktor Andreyev will come looking for me and they've got assassins everywhere.' Alice reached into the pocket of her leather jacket and handed Watts a fistful of bullets.

'You're full of surprises. Where did you get these?'

'A giant called Stretch, who is really called Rolf Steiner. Andreyev's personal bodyguard.'

'Anything else?'

'No. Just Sparrow's death. Like I said, the rest of my words were made up bollocks. I'm only reporting the one thing.'

'What's this Sparrow business really about?' asked Watts.

'It's a gift for Angelina. She's the sister I never had. I am gifting her Viktor Andreyev's head on a plate.'

'Who is Viktor Andreyev?'

FORTY-SEVEN

Baltic Power's Viktor Andreyev was an angry small man. The opposite of a gentle giant. Anger was his energy. It helped him get up in the morning. He hated anyone not from his Ukrainian homeland that had been stolen by Nazis: Africans, Americans, Australians, Asians, Albanians, Algerians, Armenians. Right through the alphabet. He hated enemies who didn't share his world views: abortionists, anarchists, assassins, activists, agitators, authors, autobiographers, agents, armies, right through the alphabet. He hated Manchester, even though he'd only been in the city for an hour. He had flown in on a private jet from the Mediterranean, where he'd been mixing business and pleasure from the sanctuary of his private yacht. He'd left behind sun, sand and lots of sex with several willing women young enough to be his granddaughters, but old enough not to get him arrested and ostracised by his fellow paper billionaires. He hated boxing, was uncomfortable witnessing violence in the flesh. Much as he hated seeing pain inflicted on people, it was an effective tactic to protect his post-perestroika business empire. Vultures were always circling high above, waiting for the opportunity to rip him to shreds. He wasn't paranoid. He knew they were out to get him. Viktor Andreyev. The former electrician who had sold virtual holocaust memorial bricks to build a Ukrainian monument that never existed. To cut a long story short, he invested the profits of imaginary bricks into buying and selling commodities and influential friends, including his equally diminutive pal, Vladimir Vladimirovich Putin.

His powerful friends helped fund and buy what became Baltic Power after a series of successful rigged auctions. His gamble to undervalue assets and spread bribes like confetti at a wedding turned millions into billions. He was astute enough to understand his continued success and protection was dependent upon keeping his allies happy with gifts that made them stronger. He constantly had to make sure he was indispensable.

Once powerful enough, he moved his business in the aftermath of the annexation of Crimea in 2014. In Germany he could legitimately trade with calmness and consistency while maintaining a high degree of anonymity. Putin liked his thinking. Russia's leader was already dreaming of restoring a three-state nation.

Remaining faceless cost Viktor a lot of money. In the early days before he could speak English, he was advised to always 'Buy British' PR, legal and accountancy services. Like the Swiss with banks full of Nazi gold and artworks, the Brits didn't care as long they could submit monthly retainer fee invoices that were as realistic as the bricks in a Jewish memorial wall that was never built.

None of this was on the record. Only a few people knew Viktor's true story. One of them was an English establishment PR consultant, Rupert Sparrow. Viktor and Rupert went back twenty-five years. Rupert pushed very occasional puff profiles in the press. Most of the time, he quietly lobbied Baltic's interests in Westminster and Europe without bigging up Viktor on the public stage.

Rupert was useful. Until he wasn't. And then Viktor ordered Stretch, Hans and Ursula to throw him out of a window and make it look like a suicide. Rupert's mistake was to panic under pressure. He had told Viktor he was being blackmailed by a government official called Ed Boucher who was armed with an establishment sex-pest list that identified dozens of British perverts.

Rupert wanted Viktor to assassinate the nominations assessor, Viktor asked why. Rupert explained about his love affair with a teenage girl, but mistakenly said, 'We all make mistakes, me shagging a schoolgirl, you best mates with Putin. If that ever leaked into the public domain, you'd lose everything. Sanctions are a killer'.

Viktor hated gamblers. He didn't like risk, so Rupert skydived on to concrete. Viktor also hated Samantha Sparrow. Standing there in front of him, so obsequious it was hard to take her seriously. He had to stop himself from spitting at her in disgust at the way she was prostituting herself. Every inch of her said she was available to be taken, used and abused. But she was old and ugly. Her porcelain false teeth too white. Her bronzed leather face had too many deep lines around the eyes. The tight bright pink cashmere cardigan showcasing slightly lopsided pear-shaped breasts that should have been fixed by a decent plastic surgeon. 'Have we got the sex-pest list?' asked Viktor. 'When am I meeting this Ed Boucher?'

'He's dead,' said Samantha.

'Like your father. Suicide?'

'Heart attack. I think.'

'And you only tell me now?'

'Better face to face. His granddaughter is going to sell us the list tonight for a fistful of uncut diamonds. I've already bought them. No connections to you.'

'Good girl,' said Viktor, impressed by her pragmatism. He was planning to sack her after the fight, but maybe she was a suitable long-term replacement for her late father. He'd already told people about the sex-pest list, keen to be seen to proactively support the war effort and assist in redrawing the map of Europe. 'Salim is happy doing the cheque presentation with me?'

'Sure. He's keen as mustard. And is open to a third fight in Riyadh with Baltic's support.'

Viktor hated people he couldn't trust, which was everyone, apart from Vlad. Putin was his mentor and spiritual guiding light. His admiration and adoration for Putin had no limits. That was why he was personally involved in buying the sex-pest list. He wanted to look into the eyes of his business partners so he would know when they were about to lose their nerve and betray him and the Russian cause.

There was an ulterior motive that he would never share, not even with

Vlad. Nothing lasted forever. Empires always imploded. The thousand-year Reich. The Soviet Union under Stalin. The British Empire ruled by public school boys who suckled by their nannies and never grew up. The rise of Viktor Andreyev would inevitably end with a fall. As long as he could postpone that day when the sky fell in on him, he was doing alright for an orphan sparks who used to wet himself as a scared teenage child alone in the dark.

Forty-eight

Angelina sat in the cab and stared at all the happy people; the women shopping; the men two steps behind, missing the pub, booze and banter and their televised sport. How many of the women had taken the same actions to remove an unwanted pregnancy? There would be stats somewhere. But she was only interested in herself. She repeated her silent mantra. Her body, her mind, her choice. If Nina had accompanied her, she would have tried to convince her to offer the child up for fostering or adoption or even consider bringing it up herself. That was Nina for you, Greek Catholic Ukrainian, believed abortion was a mortal sin. Owen had no such qualms; his presence was strangely reassuring.

The cab arrived outside the abortion clinic. A group of Christians chanted, waving wooden crosses and burning incense and candles. They gave up their leisure to show their displeasure about matters that didn't concern them. They would never understand why abortion was a right for women, until it happened to them or their children or their grandchildren. If they were raped, they would think and act differently. Hypocrites always did.

Owen walked sword side, shielding Angelina from the pro-life anti-abortionists. His right hand gripped hers, pulled her closer to him. There was tension in every muscle of his body. He carried four packs of sanitary towels.

Packed inside his rucksack were her pyjamas, a dressing gown and slippers from the Malmaison hotel. Inside his head there was a white noise riot he struggled to contain.

A nurse introduced herself as Cathy Moore and booked Angelina in. She took a few personal and medical details, and ran through her options. Angelina cut her short, said she wanted the option to have treatment that day. Cathy nodded, and said they would use the 'manual vacuum aspiration' method. The doctor would suction the pregnancy away.

They scanned her stomach. She was two days short of fourteen weeks. They checked her blood pressure. She spoke to the doctor performing the procedure and the wait began.

Three hours before the op, Cathy inserted prostaglandin tablets into Angelina's vagina to soften the neck of her womb. Pain killers were given an hour before.

Angelina emptied her bladder. She thanked Owen for his help and said she would see him shortly. Owen nodded and said he had some calls to make now he was no longer deceased. There were bridges to rebuild with his ex-wife and his rehired agent.

In the examination room Angelina's legs were suspended in stirrups. A small speculum was inserted and a local anaesthetic was injected into the cervix. The pregnancy was silently removed.

Afterwards, Angelina lay there smiling. The uninvited son or daughter was gone. Andrei Orlov's bloodline would not taint the world. 'Go fuck yourself Russian soldier. Go fuck yourself Putin.'

'Pardon?' asked Cathy Moore.

'Kissing goodbye to a memory,' said Angelina.

Five minutes later, Cathy escorted Angelina into the clinic's waiting room. Owen had company. Alice was sitting with him. She was reading Danuta Reah's The Last Room. They smiled when they saw her, no words needed. He had disobeyed her instructions on the Humber Bridge about keeping it skin deep. Putin and his enablers like Viktor Andreyev would never win.

Forty-nine

The briefing room was full of detectives, intelligence operators, counter terrorist officers and armed response, trying to make sense of what Watts had briefed them about Alice's video. His ownership of the initial Sparrow intelligence became irrelevant once it escalated to higher pay grades. The decisions of what they could do and when had nothing to do with him. Watts listened to the heavy-duty brigade discuss the merits of where to arrest the trio. They had been identified as Hans Becker and Ursula Bonn, who worked in Baltic Power's international affairs department, and Baltic's head of security, Rolf Steiner, nicknamed Stretch. Would it be better at the Arena in front of thousands, at their hotels, or travelling between the two venues? They had a small timeframe. If they missed their window, the suspects would be gone. The intelligence officers talked about Andreyev having access to his own private plane at Manchester Airport. The murderers could easily slip out unnoticed.

Watts left the room for a comfort break. The detail of the arrests wasn't relevant to him. His job was to chaperone Alice Lamb-Percy to a police station, where terrorism detectives would take her witness statement. Watts had taped an unofficial version on his mobile while the two of them sat outside the abortion clinic. She had spilled the beans. Promised not to go batshit crazy on him. But he wasn't one hundred percent sure he could trust her word. Had she played him? He'd never know, until it was too late and he was up shit creek without a paddle.

Outside the briefing room, Sir Richard shared a coffee with Carol Cox and a couple of his assistant chief constables. He would make the final decision when to arrest the terrorists. They were on his patch. They acknowledged each other, but didn't stop to chat. The chief was probably offering his senior colleagues cleansing jobs in the Middle East, the magic gift dispenser.

Watts went to the canteen and found an empty table away from off-duty traffic officers unwinding with a brew. He logged in online to send John Budd's dodgy gambling winnings to Owen Chard. But there was a problem, both of John's online gambling accounts were closed. He called his tech whizz Cassie Holmes and told her what had happened. Asked if there was a simple logical solution to follow the cash. She said would check and get back to him as soon as she found anything out. He asked her to check Shannon Quinn's socials for Friday, 25th June 2021 and two or three days either side. See what she was up to online.

Next, he called John Budd's healthcare trust fund treasurer, Marty Cohen. According to Hurst they were primed to release the funds to save Budd's name. Except they weren't. 'Sorry Nigel. All spending from the fund is blocked,' said Marty.

'Says who?'

'John's wife.'

'I'm a trustee. How come I wasn't told?'

'There are only three signatories on the bank account. Sir Richard, Heather and me. Heather called me. Said the money stays where it is. I spoke to Sir Richard. He said go with her wishes. It's hers and John's money.'

Watts called Shannon Quinn on her mobile and it went straight to voicemail. He said he wanted to book a cab to take him to the boxing tonight, but already knew she wouldn't call back, unlike Cassie, who rang him half an hour later with predictable news. Apparently photographs and social media posts had Shannon Quinn in the Lakes with her kids and her mum on Friday 25th June, 2021. Cassie had reopened the two closed online betting accounts. Seventy grand from the RedORBlack account had been sent to Heather's personal bank account. The twenty grand at Sunshine had brightened up Shannon's day. The money had been transferred from both accounts late Friday night, minutes after he'd spoken to Heather.

Watts went back online and accessed the portal with the folders cataloguing the Zara Abi kidnapping evidence. Was Heather lying about the rings too? She said she had found them in John's belongings. The hospital had given them to her once John Budd was in theatre undergoing surgery. There were no rings logged among John's belongings, apart from his wedding band. The investigating team had done half the job. He couldn't blame them. He'd never have thought John Budd had organised the kidnapping or involved his own wife. Never looked at the evidence in that context.

Watts left the canteen with a coffee and went back to the corridor outside the briefing room. The chief constable was still joking with Carol Cox. Should Watts tell Hurst and let somebody else make the decisions?

'Nigel.'

'Chief.'

'Good work with the Russians. The force will be making headlines for the right reasons when they arrest them. Good intelligence.'

'Thank you. A private word about you know who.'

'No need for privacy. Carol told me about the mix up over the identities of Owen Chard and Ed Boucher. Is it all contained?'

'I think so.'

'Carol showed me the timelines. We never met Ed Boucher. She didn't. You didn't. I didn't. We don't want to look like imbeciles.'

'Who did we meet?'

'I'm disappointed in you Nigel. That's a flippant question,' said Hurst.

'Sorry.'

'The Cabinet Office will send up another nominations assessor. Hopefully he stays alive long enough to give John Budd his gong.'

This was the one opportunity to tell the chief, but Watts couldn't find the words. Whatever he said, Hurst would stonewall him into submission. Fuck justice. This was a private matter between him and his former best friend who turned to be a corrupt cunt alongside his equally culpable wife. 'When are you making the arrests?' asked Watts.

'We're not going to arrest the terrorists until after the fight. If we do it before, the boxing will be called off. We'll look ridiculous in front of the entire world.'

Watts nodded and walked away from the chief and the PR girl. They casually resumed their conversation, unbothered by the mess swilling around their feet. Hurst would probably take her to the Middle East with him. Somebody should tell Hurst's wife, but there was an unwritten honour code among thieves, serial adulterers and police officers. What happened on the bed, stayed on the bed.

Out of earshot, Watts called Owen. Told him there was no money on the table. The chief knew about Boucher's death and somebody impersonating the dead man. If it was contained, Owen and Angelina and Alice could walk from Manchester free people.

'No money at all?' asked Owen.

'Be grateful you're not locked up,' replied Watts. 'You could always put a bet on Muller to KO Juke in the fourth round.'

'From the horse's mouth?'

'The same source that predicted the last result,' said Watts.

'Are you betting?'

'I don't gamble. Is Alice with you?'

'Yes,' replied Owen.

'Tell her I'll need an official statement tomorrow. She knows what I mean,' said Watts.

'See you at the boxing,' said Owen.

'I've got another job to do,' said Watts.

FIFTY

No money, said Watts. Have a gamble on a boxing match instead. The whole blackmail gig had imploded. To get so far, so near, so close and to fail. It reminded him of Beckett's quote about failing, trying again and failing better. This failure would make his memoirs newsworthy when he penned them in a couple of years' time. He'd have to repair the relationship with his agent Charlie Wolff first. Even though he'd explained a dozen times, Charlie was still upset by Angelina's comments. Same as Owen's ex-wife, who was relieved he was still alive for the kids' sake, disappointed that the potty mouthed trollop had said what she said and lied about remarrying.

'What, no money?' asked Alice in their hotel room.

Angelina was lying on the bed dozing. Alice was packing up her grandfather's belongings. Separating Ed's things from Owen's. 'He says we should be grateful we're not locked up,' said Owen.

'He's got a point,' said Alice. She delved into Angelina's jeans, found her lighter, grabbed her own mobile and the rape allegation letter. 'Follow me.' In the en suite, she closed the door. Dismantled the smoke alarm. Held the rape allegation letter over the sink. Lit it. Watched it burn rapidly.

'Was it true?' asked Owen.

'Yes.'

'Who?'

'A secret. She needs space to rebuild. Her compensation will help.'

'There isn't any money.'

'Putin can help pay.'

'Pay? What do you mean?'

'At the boxing we'll sell him Ed's sex-pest list before we go on holiday.'

'Holiday?'

'Are you going to repeat my every last word?'

Back in the main hotel room, Alice woke Angelina and explained that they needed to recuperate from their recent experiences. She had access to a villa in Thailand and would pay them to join her at a writer's workshop for a couple of weeks. They could work on songs, short stories or a novel together. Write a film script. Anything, as long as it wasn't autobiographical. That was too painful. Nobody would find it interesting. 'We can fly out tonight. Before the boxing, we cash in our lottery ticket. I've got some admin to do first and then we'll go.' She called three contacts in the south. The first was Ed's line manager at the Cabinet Office to say she would post back the John Budd files. The next was Ed's solicitor to inform her about the death. She said the funeral would have to wait until the police released the body. Finally, she called Irene, her grandmother, at the nursing home and spoke to her briefly through the dementia fog. When Alice finished, she requested an answer about Asia. Angelina said she wanted to get back to Ukraine to join the war against Putin. 'You deserve recuperation time,' said Alice. 'We all do.'

'Who is going to pay for all this?' asked Owen.

'Perverts,' replied Alice.

'Why should we trust you?'

'Because I'm survivor. And so are you. And so is Angelina,' said Alice. She explained, paraphrasing her abuse at the hands of Ed and Irene into a five-minute monologue.

Angelina followed her, talked about Bucha without going into graphic detail. Owen felt he had nothing to compare to the two women and then found that the words flowed from him too. 'Music and TV and the film industries abuse you, with money men mugging you off. They offer you hope and great expectations and then whip them away just when you think the world is about to be your oyster. This blackmail gig was the same.' They sat in silence and contemplated what each of them had said.

'I'll go,' said Angelina.

'You?' asked Alice.

'I'm in,' said Owen. The two weeks away from the UK would allow him to reboot.

'Let's go to the boxing and hope Andreyev's security team has been dismantled,' said Alice.

'What do you mean?' asked Owen.

'The police are arresting some of his bodyguards. He won't be as cocky without them.'

'Go fuck yourself, Viktor,' said Angelina, grinning.

Fifty-one

Watts watched from his car, parked halfway down the avenue. He had a clear sight of the green door on the mid-terrace. At eight thirty a limousine arrived. He watched Heather and Hannah climb into the car wearing matching white cocktail dresses. Hannah was a younger, thinner spit of her mother. He saw them drive off. Half an hour later the live-in care left, scurrying down the avenue for a secret rendezvous with an online lover. Sneaking out, leaving her patient without the 24-hour care his medical needs demanded.

Watts got out of his car, walked up the avenue, and let himself in through the front door. All the alarm systems were switched off. Not just the alarms, all the electricity too. Silently, he crept around the ground floor and checked each room was empty. John Budd was asleep in his room. Watts pulled up a chair and removed the pillow placed on it. He sat beside his oldest friend. 'Hi John.' Watts used his mobile to connect to the boxing on his PayPerView app. 'Let's watch the boxing.' There was an hour or so until the big fight started. Talking heads hyped up the fight and said JJ had a puncher's chance, but the bigger man was always more likely to win than a smaller chap. 'Shall we place a bet? I can afford to lose a grand.'

Watts placed a thousand pounds online on Muller to knock out Juke in the fourth round at odds of thirty-three to one. Had Owen done the same thing? Watts watched the small mobile screen, the sound turned down low. He didn't want to spook the house visitor that would be popping in soon. The TV showed highlights from the first fight he and Budd had missed. Watts thought JJ looked good, regretted the grand on the fourth. There was a tugging on his arm, the man who couldn't control his bowel movements or his tongue was trying to communicate with him.

'What do you want?'

'Do it now. Please. No more,' said the man who hadn't communicated to anyone for twelve months.

Watts silenced the mobile and turned to face John. Tears were streaming down Budd's face and his hand shook as he tried to grip the detective's arm. Watts heard the door open. A dark shadow stood in the entrance. He couldn't see the face, but he knew it was. 'Hi Shannon. You never told me Heather was the "third man". Did she pay you to take the blame for the kidnapping or to finish the job of killing John Budd?'

'Both. Twenty grand buys a uni education. We all know what John wants.'

Watts knew she was right. Whatever his faults, he had to put his friend first. John had no life. If the shoe was on the other foot, JB would do the same for him, no questions asked. 'Me before you?'

'One either side,' said Shannon, who took the pillow from Watts and placed it over John's head.

FIFTY-TWO

Stretch grinned at Alice as she led Owen and Angelina into the back office of the Baltic VIP area in the Manchester Arena. Two of his operatives patted them down and found Owen's betting slip and said five grand on Muller to knock out Jones in the fourth round was madness. Juke would be lucky to survive three minutes. They declared the trio clean and allowed them to enter the suite.

Alice wondered why Stretch was running free. He should have been arrested by now.

There were two doors. One led into the hospitality area where Alice could see liggers lapping up Baltic hospitality. The other door led to a boardroom. Stretch winked several times at Alice and she winked back salaciously: if only you knew, you murdering bastard. Stretch left.

They sat in the room in silence. Like they were at a funeral, Alice, Owen and Angelina in mourning. A beat or two passed. The crowd roared from the arena. The doors opened.

Hans Becker and Ursula Bonn entered, followed by the two giants and a returning Stretch. Last in was Viktor Andreyev, the smallest person in the room, despite the shoe lifts. Viktor sat at the top of the table and stared straight at Alice. 'I am sorry to hear about the death of your grandfather,' said Viktor.

'I'm not,' replied Alice.

'Who are your friends? Are you going to introduce them?'

'No. We're going on holiday. A writer's retreat.'

'Nice work if you can get it,' said Viktor. 'Ursula, give her the diamonds. Your list please, Alice.'

A small box was pushed across the table to Alice who diverted them to Owen. He looked inside and nodded. Alice took an A4 envelope from her handbag and started to push it towards Ursula. Then she stopped and opened the envelope and pulled out the top sheet. 'I'll read them out to you.'

Russian agent Alexander Litvinenko, died of polonium-210 poisoning in London in 2006.

Russian journalist Anna Politkovskaya, killed outside her flat in Moscow, returning home from the supermarket in 2006.

Opposition leader Boris Nemtsov, shot four times in the back by an unknown assailant within view of the Kremlin in 2015.

Georgian citizen Zelimkhan Khangoshvili, shot twice in the head at close range in Kleiner Tiergarten, a park in central Berlin in 2019.

Putin critic Boris Berezovsky, found hanged in the bathroom of his Ascot home in 2013.

'Stop,' demanded Andreyev.

'You wanted the list,' said Alice. 'You paid for it.'

Mikhail Lesin discovered dead in a hotel room in Washington DC in 2015.

Politician Sergei Yushenkov, shot in front of his Moscow home in 2003.

Natalya Estemirova, killed with bullet wounds to her head and chest, found in Ingushetia, hours after her abduction near her home in the capital of Chechnya, Grozny.

Lawyer Sergei Magnitsky, died in police custody, November 2009, after allegedly being brutally beaten, then denied medical care.

English political lobbyist, Rupert Sparrow, pushed from a fourth-floor window by three people in this room in 2022. My birth father.

'And finally,' said Alice.

Baltic Power energy boss, Viktor Andreyev, plane crash in 2024.

Alice glanced at Angelina. If her eyes were lasers, they would have burned a hole straight through Andreyev's ice-cold heart. 'You English have a very strange sense of humour. Do you want to join the death list you've read out?' asked Viktor.

'You before me,' grinned Alice. 'Putin's paranoid enough and there's only one reason you avoided sanctions, because you're snitching to the USA and the west.'

'Rubbish.'

'Not me you have to convince,' said Alice. 'My grandfather Ed Boucher told me about you and Rupert and Putin. It's been passed all down the spook line. Your day in the sun will come, my friend.'

'Born in Ukraine yet you have no shame or conscience. A bullet has your name on it, Viktor Andreyev,' said Angelina. 'Maybe not today or tomorrow, but one day. A bullet is the only language traitors like you understand. You won't hear it until it hits you, tiny man.'

'You're talking to the right man,' said Owen, clapping his hands and laughing.

Viktor snarled and they laughed at the little big man. Viktor motioned to Stretch to take back the box of uncut stones. Stretch moved towards them, but Alice shouted for him to stop. 'Leave.'

Stretch did as he was told. Alice said she had removed the bullets from his gun. He was too slack and shagged to check on his weapon. She said she had done it last night when they fucked like rabbits. While he snored, she emptied his magazine. The police had the bullets as evidence with his prints all over the ammo.

'Viktor, we'll have your diamonds. Bring me a laptop and I'll give you access to the sex-pest list. You can blackmail as many child abusers as you want. I never offered them my protection and their guardian angel has popped his clogs. But your three assassins who murdered my shit yellow dad better run fast. The cops are coming, if they don't like jail.'

FIFTY-THREE

The cops never did turn up. Somebody from London, right at the top of the food chain, pulled the raid. But the fuckers ran with their tails between their legs, the look of panic on all their faces was priceless. Viktor never even presented the cheque, the PR money shot blown by their collective paranoia.

'Run rabbits run,' said Alice, as they fled the room and the arena. 'The wolves are never far away.'

AFTER
FRIDAY 22ND NOVEMBER 2024

John Budd was awarded a posthumous George Cross. His wife Heather and daughter Hannah went to Buckingham Palace to receive the bravery medal from the King. John had passed peacefully in his sleep almost two and a half years earlier on the same night Wolfgang Muller knocked out Juke JJ Jones in the fourth round of their world title fight in Manchester. JJ lost the trilogy rematch in Saudi Arabia a year later.

The medal ceremony was on the national six o'clock news. Heather Budd and Hannah posed for the media outside the palace gates with retired chief constable Sir Richard Hurst, the George Cross and glasses of champagne. Off camera, Heather was joined by her new husband-to-be, a YouTube fitness influencer several years her junior. Hannah's boyfriend was waiting in the wings, a European student and blues guitar picker called Laurent from Paris, France. The duo was studying for Psychology degrees at UCL. Hannah lived in London. Her mother had moved down south to be nearer to her.

Nigel Watts watched the coverage on the TV in his front room. It made a change to view a 'good news' story amid the constant stream of child sex abuse allegations faced by politicians and celebrities caught with their big boy pants around their ankles. Nigel knew the truth, but kept his mouth zipped. He had retired from the police force and was planning to fly out to Japan with his wife Frankie, who was speaking at a conference on false memory syndrome in Tokyo.

Watts volunteered in his free time, mentoring teenagers who didn't understand the dangers of serious crime and bad company. He encouraged the youngsters to take up boxing rather than knives. Harry Quinn, struggling with prostate cancer, let Nigel use his gym for free and provided kit for nowt.

Was Watts making a difference?

If he stopped one person from screwing up their lives, it justified all his bad decisions. Taking Heather down would have ruined Hannah's life, and the poor girl deserved better. Heather gave him the rings in return for his silence. She promised to leave Manchester, never to return or contact him again. Watts threw the Arab rings into the water at Salford Quays. They were cursed and were responsible for too many deaths. One day somebody might find them and claim the reward. Good luck to them. They'd need it.

Shannon Quinn was reading to her fifth child as she watched the news. She whispered to her daughter she was going to have a better life than her mum and the dead brother she would never meet. Shannon said she'd had Paul too young. Didn't understand motherhood as a teen. Kirsty would benefit from the lessons learned through her mother's bitter experience. She had a university fund to free her from the poverty trap. Her horizons wouldn't be blurred by class or lack of money.

Samantha Sparrow, Viktor Andreyev and Rolf 'Stretch' Steiner died in a plane crash in the winter of 2022. Apparently, their Learjet lost cabin pressure. All six passengers and the crew were incapacitated by hypoxia, a lack of oxygen in the brain and body. The plane carried on flying for almost four hours and fifteen hundred miles before running out of fuel and crashing into the Kara Sea. None of the bodies were recovered. The Kremlin denied any responsibility for the 'accident'. The British intelligence services denied Andreyev or Sparrow worked for them, as did the Americans, but the world would never know the truth until the spooks involved retired and started writing their memoirs to supplement substantial pensions.

Alice Lamb-Percy saw the posthumous Budd award news online. Later, she zoomed former staff nurse Sally Marsh and checked she was OK that her abuser was back in the public eye. Sally said she was still taking it day by day and every time she went to bed alive was a small victory. Knowing John Budd was dead didn't make her recovery any easier, like she had thought it would. Some things you could never get over. Alice agreed. The money for ongoing therapy helped.

Alice was in the USA, discussing film distribution deals with the streamers. She'd set up a film production company with her business partner, former actor Owen Chard. The duo commuted between offices and studios in Thailand and Hampshire. They specialised in animated movies for kids and had released two features to date, with two more in production. In her spare time, Alice managed a UK charity for abused kids. Victims of abuse were offered holidays at her villa in Bangkok, complemented by therapy sessions in England based on a programme devised and led by Frankie Watts. Nigel had contacted Owen and Alice when they returned from Thailand and introduced them to his wife. Alice told everyone Owen was her mentor and guiding light, he kept her sane when the wild winds blew too hard.

Owen was doing post-production work at an animation studio in Sheffield as he watched the posthumous awards clip on Sky TV. Alice had given him a reason to get up in the mornings, but he was always waiting for the inevitable, he could tell. Brave as she was, she was always hiding the pain cutting could never truly mask. The damage of her youth was permanent. The memories too deep. One day they would catch her by surprise. He hoped somebody would be there to snatch her from the sky before she splattered. Until then, they co-existed, almost like siblings. All the videos from Manchester had been destroyed. Only those who saw them at the time would ever know they had existed. Occasionally, Alice would say sorry for having had Owen without consent. He would laugh it off with a joke about not having dinner first. But most of the time he blotted out the memory and focused on their shared love of the creativity they had unleashed in each other.

As well as films, he occasionally gigged, resurrecting Vic Savage minus his savage sheep. His audience had grown old with him and wallowed in their shared nostalgia.

On the day John Budd got his George Cross, Owen gigged in Newcastle. Late at night, he diverted sixty miles east down the M62 from the A1/M1. He drove to the Humber Bridge to say goodbye to a good friend who had died on 25th April 2024, day 789 of Russia's illegal invasion of Ukraine. It was time to say farewell properly.

Angelina Kozar was killed in the eastern Donbas region during a counter-offensive.

She had initially gone back as a frontline nurse as Ukraine tried to repel the invaders, but she felt impotent healing, not hurting, especially when she found out about the death of Viktor Andreyev. She put away the uniform and retrained as a sniper. Her goal was to force the invaders to leave one by one, either on foot or in a body bag. Her confirmed kill list was twice her age and then some. Alice and Owen had delivered emergency aid to Ukraine several times on behalf of Nina Mazur. They begged Angelina to stay safe and remove herself from the front line.

She refused.

'We didn't come to them with a war. They came to us. Raped us and our land. I wasn't saved from a bridge to cook borscht and cry for the bereaved. If I can abort my own child's life against every instinct, I can shoot the invaders who steal my freedom. Our freedom. Your freedom.'

Nina told Owen about Angelina's death without shedding tears. She was immune to suffering. She advised Owen to avoid images of Angelina's dead body in a potato field, and Russians bragging on social media and Owen stayed well clear. Nina said Angelina's body was recovered and buried in Bucha next to her husband Marko, his brother Borden and their cousin Symon.

Bumping into Angelina on the bridge had saved Owen and given him a new life. He hadn't been able to return the favour, as hard as he'd tried. She hadn't even made thirty years of age, but she died with her boots on, doing herself and her country proud.

Alone, late at night, Owen walked out to the middle of the Humber Bridge humming the Stones' *Wild Horses*. Let's do some living, before we die.

Not any longer.

He carried a red balloon with the postmodern ironic *CUTE BUT 101% PSYCHO* slogan printed on the side. There would be no Lofoten island trips accompanied by a beautiful soul with striking red hair and light blue-green eyes. No free-falling into the unknown.

He'd broken his promise about keeping everything skin deep. He hoped she would forgive him and understand. It was always an impossible ask once they let each other into their lives. Humans had to care for each other. There was no other way to survive as a species.

Owen let the balloon go and watched it float high into the cold, moonlit night.

Like a smoke ring.

He watched it for as long as he could before it disappeared into space for an eternity. He would never know the truth of its journey. Could only guess.

'Wherever you are Angelina Kozar tonight, I hope, to quote Alice, you're catching water in a net.'